JOHN HENRY BERNARD

1860–1927

John Henry Bernard
1860–1927

A study of a leader of the southern unionists

———————

R.B. MacCARTHY

LINDEN
Publishing Services

Published in 2008 by

LINDEN PUBLISHING LTD • DUBLIN • IRELAND

Cover portrait of John Henry Bernard, by C. Hall Neale, from the Cashel & Ossory
diocesan portrait collection.
(Courtesy of RCB Library, Dublin)
Back cover portrait of Bernard by Dr Whelan
(Courtesy of Trinity College, Dublin)

ISBN: 978 1 905487 21 9

Bernard papers have been consulted courtesy of the British Library
and the Board of Trinity College Dublin.
A generous grant in aid of publication from the
General Synod of the Church of Ireland is acknowledged.

This book is typeset in Adobe Caslon 11.5 on 14 point Quadraat
Designed by Susan Waine
Printed and bound in Great Britain by MPG Books, Bodmin, Cornwall

Contents

Foreword

THIS MONOGRAPH does not aim to cover every aspect of John Henry Bernard's life.

It does not deal with his family life – he married his cousin Maud Nannie Bernard in 1885[1] and they had two sons and two daughters. Nor does it deal with his claims to scholarship in the fields of history and theology;[2] nor with his roles as warden of Alexandra College or president of the Royal Irish Academy (1919–21).

R.H. Murray's book *Archbishop Bernard* published in 1931 is in no sense a critical biography but it is useful because it prints *in extenso* various tributes which were paid to Bernard following his death.

—ɷ—

Introduction

JOHN HENRY BERNARD was born in India in 1860 as a very impoverished Irish Protestant. His father was by descent one of the Bernards of Kerry – about whom the future archbishop was to write a book – but he died in 1863 as an engineer on the Indian railways leaving his widow to bring up his son and daughter in extremely straitened circumstances; their only asset was his life insurance of £2,000 and she had about £80 p.a. to live on – so straitened in fact that John Henry had to pay his way though Trinity College by acting as a junior master at Rathmines School.

He went to school for the first time in January 1870 – to a day school in Bray where he and his mother lived. The headmaster was an ex-scholar of Trinity College named Mr Courtenay. Five years later when he went to be headmaster of St John's College, Newport, Co. Tipperary, Bernard went with him as a boarder for a few months before he entered Trinity College. St John's College has long ceased to exist and has been described as "a small struggling school under the Incorporated Society for Promoting Protestant Schools in Ireland".[3] One suspects that its main advantage in the eyes of Mrs Bernard was that it was cheap. Obviously Bernard did not enjoy the experience and he described his school fellows as "rough country louts who took pleasure in badgering anyone inferior to them in strength".[4]

He entered Trinity College Dublin at what was even then the unusually young age of 15 and in spite of that he won first place at entrance and he continued to live with his mother and sister at Bray. His undergraduate course was a very brilliant one. He became a Scholar in 1879 with the highest marks on record and he graduated in 1880 with the second senior moderatorship in mathematics and mathematical physics and the second senior moderatorship in mental and moral philosophy.

He then began to work for a prize fellowship which was then the only means of obtaining a teaching fellowship in the college. He competed at the examinations for fellowship in 1882, 1883 and 1884 and he finally won in 1884, the runner-up being the great historian John Bury who was elected in the following year. It was a particularly brilliant circle which Bernard now joined and he found his friends mostly among classical scholars and theologians such as Mahaffy, Bury, FitzGerald, Gwynn and Salmon.[5]

—ɯ—

The Churchman

JOHN HENRY BERNARD was ordained in 1886 on the title of his fellowship and was the first since disestablishment in 1869 to do so. In the same year he was elected to assist John Gwynn, the Archbishop King's lecturer in divinity. The head of the divinity school at this time was George Salmon, the Regius Professor of Divinity. In 1888 Salmon became provost, Gwynn succeeded him in the regius chair and Salmon supported Bernard for the Archbishop King's lectureship – it was really far more than a lectureship since the lecturer had charge of the junior divinity year and it formally became a chair in 1906. In spite of being only 27 years of age and having never served in a parish, Bernard was elected against a strong field – Dr Travers Smith and Dr Charles Wright were also candidates. Provost Salmon gave him his casting vote and Salmon's friendship and support was to be very important to him in the years ahead. It was no doubt due to Salmon, who was the chancellor, that Dean Jellett appointed him treasurer of St Patrick's in 1897 or that the chapter elected him dean in 1902 at the early age of 42. Meanwhile he gave his lectures in the divinity school and quickly gained the admiration of the students there – at that time there were generally over 100 men in the divinity school and half of them would have been under Bernard in the junior year. Indeed, the 1,150 men who had passed through Bernard's hands into the ministry of the church between 1888 and his resignation on being made a bishop in 1911 were foremost in their appreciation of all that he had to give to the church. He wasn't just a lecturer – he played a large part in the social life of his students. As well as encouraging the Theological Society, he contributed to its debates night by night each term. As if this was not enough, he and Professor Cunningham took over the whole organisation of the tercentenary celebrations in 1892 which occupied a whole week including a great service at St Patrick's.

According to the college historians "he was one of those young men who are fortunate enough to be respected and trusted alike by their seniors and their contemporaries. As a prominent member of the reform party in college he was keen and resolute but never shrill and never too rigid to consider a possible compromise and he made no enemies in controversy."[6]

All the while, from 1888 to 1904, even though Provost Salmon had admitted him to his intimacy, Bernard used to "watch with anxiety the methods by which college business was transacted. Truth to tell I was wholly dissatisfied with the way in which college business was administered. Reform of the college was ardently desired by several of the junior fellows and professors and "by none more than myself."[7] Provost Salmon's rule was "very arbitrary and he was intolerant of all new ideas – he often spoke in caustic terms of the contest for the provostship which would be waged after his death by Mahaffy and Traill."[8] But in fact Bernard was also very seriously considered for the post which was in the gift of the crown and the prime minister could nominate whoever he wished.

Bernard was the candidate recommended by the Lord Lieutenant, the Earl of Dudley, while the Revd J.P. Mahaffy was the candidate of the Chief Secretary, George Wyndham, because, it was said, he was the only fellow to support Wyndham's scheme for including Trinity College in a new federal university for Ireland. Why then did Anthony Traill secure the appointment? Largely because of what were perceived as deficiencies in the other two candidates. Both were clergymen and it was thought that a lay provost would have a better chance of defusing Catholic hostility to Trinity College.

Much has been made of the fact that Bernard was no longer a fellow but in fact he held precisely the same qualifications as George Salmon, the late provost, had at his appointment – both were ex-fellows actively engaged as professors in the divinity school. Bernard himself believed that "Traill slipped in between Mahaffy and me because he had the Orangemen in the House of Commons in his pocket just at the moment when their votes were needed by the government".[9] None of these reasons was adverted to by the prime minister in a letter to George Wyndham on 26 February 1904. Having initially said that Traill was impossible Arthur Balfour spelled out why he was nevertheless nominating him for the provostship. He pointed out that the great mass of graduate opinion, resident and non-resident was distinctly even violently hostile to Mahaffy. He went on to admit that Bernard was the more distinguished man but that Traill would be more acceptable to the fellows. He believed that he had played a very useful part in the business affairs of the college and also "he has money of his own."[10] With the benefit of hindsight, Bernard was able to write in 1919, "It was really a good thing for me that I was not made provost in 1904. I should have broken my heart trying to carry reforms which would have been blocked at every stage by the jealousy and conservatism of the older men and I should probably have failed to do much good."[11]

As well as a steady stream of articles, Bernard developed a gift for organisation and administration which came to the fore during his years as dean of St Patrick's (1902–11). As Newport White has written: "his duties in the divinity school continued of course to be discharged faultlessly: but his heart was now at St Patrick's ... at no period were the cathedral services rendered with more correctness and solemnity ..."[12] But Newport White did not publish his own critical view of Bernard's decision to forsake the college, as he saw it, for the deanery of St Patrick's. "It was a wearisome thing waiting for dead men's shoes" was how Bernard put it to White, and White's son, George (Bernard's godson), told the present writer that it was to his father as if St Francis of Assisi had calmly sat down to discuss his career prospects.

Bernard's account of his election as dean is fascinating for its matter-of-factness: "The chapter met and elected me as their dean. I got 13 votes to Dean Dickinson's 10. I spent the afternoon at the cathedral with Col. Addison (Lord Iveagh's secretary) looking over the restoration work. It is a great trust and responsibility."[13] He had clearly been Salmon's candidate – Salmon even going so far as to hold a dinner at the provost's house on the night before the election "to meet the chapter of St Patrick's" as Bernard put it.[14] There was a full turn-out of the chapter and what is therefore surprising is that the election was so close – the defeated candidate was 75 years of age and retired in the same year from both the deanery of the Chapel Royal and the vicarage of St Ann's.

Bernard by comparison was aged 42 and at the height of his powers, which were now put at the disposal of St Patrick's for the next nine years. Clearly the relationship with the Guinness family, the munificent restorers of St Patrick's, would be crucial, and Lord Iveagh and the young dean became firm friends. This was the first earl who between 1899 and 1904 carried through a complete restoration of the choir and built the present organ chamber – not to mention £250,000 on the replacement of slum dwellings around the cathedral – while his father had between 1860 and 1865 spent £150,000 on the nave and transepts. The first fruits of Bernard's friendship with Lord Iveagh came with the gift of 4000 guineas for restoration work in 1903. On Friday 24 July in that year King Edward VII visited the cathedral: "I walked round the building with him. In the evening I was at a party at the Vice-Regal Lodge – a fine night – had a word or two with the queen." Electric light was installed in the cathedral in 1910.

Bernard was almost always present at matins and evensong daily in the cathedral and we get in his diary one or two snap-shots of the huge numbers which on occasions might be present. On Christmas Eve 1903 he noted "an immense congregation to hear the Christmas carols after Evensong" and on the following day "2,800 people at Evensong". (It is doubtful if the cathedral would hold that number!) On Easter Day 1906 he preached at both matins and evensong and noted laconically "usual crowds". After the Dublin Diocesan Synod that year he had occasion to write: "they put me off

the list of Diocesan Nominators in revenge for the election to canon-
ries at St Patrick's".

He used his position at St Patrick's to strengthen the links
between the churches of England and Ireland. He was a frequent
visitor across the water – he was select preacher at both Oxford and
Cambridge and on Good Friday 1906 he took the Three Hours at St
Mary Abbot's, Kensington, with about 1,500 in the congregation.
The following Good Friday he was at All Saints, Ennismore
Gardens. In June 1906 he preached on disestablishment in
Westminster Abbey and also preached what he describes as "a very
poor sermon" at Eton. It was as a result of a sermon in Westminster
Abbey in 1911, attended by members of the Russian Duma, that he
was included in a parliamentary delegation to Russia in 1912.

Royal occasions always drew great crowds to St Patrick's. On
the Sunday after King Edward died he preached to "nearly 3,000"
at evensong. He said that the organisation of the memorial service
took a fortnight out of his life – not the least of his problems was the
Lord Lieutenant, Lord Aberdeen, whom he described as "an absurd
person although very kind in his foolish way". On the day of the
service he rose at 5 a.m. (6 a.m. the previous day) and was able to
describe the service as "the finest thing of the kind I ever saw. I am
thankful it is all over and that it was impressive and devout." In the
following year the new king, George V, paid a state visit to Ireland
and Bernard clearly took pleasure in receiving the royal family at St
Patrick's during his last weeks as dean. The primate preached and
there were 2,300 people present.

He made himself something of an expert on his great predecessor Jonathan Swift. In 1912 he gave the discourse in Trinity week on
"The discontent of Dean Swift" and he gathered in the deanery
house many memorabilia of the great dean including his Chinese
cabinet originally willed to his niece Mrs Whiteway; Bernard now
got up a subscription to purchase it from her heirs. He also obtained
Swift's snuff box which he persuaded the Lord Lieutenant, Lord
Dudley, to purchase at auction and present to the deanery.

In 1911 this strenuous and very public ministry in Dublin came
to an end with his appointment by the House of Bishops as Bishop

of Ossory, Ferns and Leighlin. Appointments were made with greater speed in those days: his successor in the deanery, Dean Ovenden of Clogher, was elected and installed on the day after Bernard's consecration. His predecessor was not pleased and noted, "I fear much that his election is not for the best interests of the cathedral." Bernard himself welcomed his departure from Dublin. He wrote "having kept 108 consecutive terms it was time to get experience outside TCD and Dublin. Kilkenny did a great deal for me in many ways."[15]

Bernard now entered on what has been described as "Four years of comparative rest"[16] at Kilkenny – despite the fact that there were at that period no less than 140 clergy in the united dioceses. Certainly the new bishop displayed what would now be regarded as a very restful approach to his episcopal duties. He was enthroned in St Canice's on 1 August 1911 and in Leighlin and Ferns on the two following days and spent some time settling into the Palace – the weekly wages were only £1.1s.0d but the removal expenses were £65! But by the week beginning 13 August he was ready to devote three whole days each week to his current writing on the *Odes of Solomon*. His main method of getting to know his new dioceses was to make week-end forays to stay with the nobility and gentry. Thus in his first two months he stayed with Lord and Lady Carew at Castle Boro, with Lord and Lady Rathdonnell at Lisnavagh, with the Earl and Countess of Desart at Desart Court,[17] with Col. Cosby at Stradbally Hall, with the Robertsons at Huntington Castle and with "Old Lord Courtown". He began to get the measure of his councils and synods: he noted with satisfaction that at the Leighlin Synod "an unmannerly motion was snuffed out". By contrast the Ossory Synod was described as "very peaceful". By the end of September the bishop and his wife were ready for a continental holiday which lasted three weeks and cost all-in £60!

Thereafter Bernard settled into the predictable round of services (daily in the cathedral), confirmations, preachments, meetings and writing letters – with, in his case, considerable time spent on his historical and theological writing. At the beginning of 1912 he noted the servants who lived in the Palace: there was a cook, a parlour-maid, a housemaid, an under-housemaid and a laundry-maid. Clearly he had already come a long way from his days as an impoverished student. The wages of all these servants amounted to just £180 p.a. whereas his episcopal stipend was £1500 p.a.

For examples of the life he led as Bishop of Ossory we can turn to his diary for 1913:[18]

At the beginning of January he instituted a new rector of Clonmantagh and motored to Carlow to preside over a board of nomination for Aghold. But he left for London on 4 January and did not return until the 13th. During most of that time he was the guest of Lord Iveagh at Elveden and then went to stay with the Earl and Countess of Desart at 2 Rutland Gardens. While there he spent a morning at the British Museum "hunting up pedigree matters" and on one Sunday attended the Temple Church after which he had lunch at the Royal Hospital, Chelsea "with the Lytteltons".

Then he spent two days in Dublin during which he attended the Representative Church Body and a bishops' meeting after which he headed back to his diocese: he was met at Mountrath station from where he was then driven to Lacca where he dedicated a new reredos, finally reaching Kilkenny at 6 p.m. Then on the 18th he and Mrs Bernard motored over to Flood Hall to stay with Major Hanford; at dinner there were Sir Hercules Langrishe, the Humphreys and the Izods. He notes that the brandy consumed dated from 1811! The following morning he preached at nearby Knocktopher church and returned to the Palace. During the remainder of the month he instituted two new incumbents in Co. Carlow and he preached in Ballyragget and Odagh (near Kilkenny). The month ended on a lighter note: "Maud, the girls and Connor motored to Waterford for the hunt ball and didn't get home until 6.45 in the morning!"

Each Sunday in February he preached at a church in his diocese on two Sundays and in St Canice's Cathedral on the other two. He notes that his wife had "20 people or so" to tea on the 13th and he lunched with Ellen Lady Desart and Lord & Lady Ormonde. He slept four days in Dublin during which he attended a bishops' meeting and the Representative Church Body; gave a lecture on Russia to the YMCA "badly attended" and spent an afternoon at the Record Office.

In March he preached at Kilrush and Newtownbarry and conducted a confirmation at Tullow. Again he spent four days in Dublin during which he preached in Christ Church, Leeson Park and lunched with the Phairs and preached in North Strand while staying with the Lewis-Crosbys in Mountjoy Square. He spent one whole day at the Record Office and Registry of Deeds and another in the college library. His only entry for Good Friday is "after a drive we had tea with the Desarts". He preached at St Canice's on Easter Day when it was back to Dublin to preach at Stirling Berry's consecration as Bishop of Killaloe on Easter Tuesday.

In April he played golf with Lord Desart and wrote sermons for the General Synod service on 14 April and for Wales – where he preached on 9 April at a united diocesan conference in Llandudno. While there he also had a talk with the Bishop of St David's about Welsh disestablishment. While attending the General Synod in Dublin he gave the address at a Girls' Friendly Society service in St Patrick's and took the chair at a lantern lecture for the Jews Society. Then on Saturday 19 April he left Dublin by train, did a confirmation at Maryborough and then motored to Stradbally to stay with Sir Hunt Walsh at Ballykilcavan. On the Sunday he attended three services there and then on the Monday went to Abbeyleix for a confirmation and a lecture on Russia in the evening.

During the rest of April four ordination candidates spent two nights at the Palace – on 23 April he notes "candidates in house all day". He presided at a meeting of the glebes and finance committee – "tiring but useful" – and then at the end of the month he and Mrs Bernard motored 52 miles to Shanbally Castle in south Tipperary to stay with Lady Constance Butler who was a daughter of the Marquess of Ormonde. They left the castle on 2 May "after a very pleasant visit".[19] Then three days were devoted to confirmations in Carlow, Baltinglass and Tinahely.

In the middle of May he was absent from Kilkenny for a week's manoeuvres; he confirmed a young farmer privately after preaching at Aghade, Co. Carlow and after a confirmation at Kiltennell he dined and slept at Borris House, the seat of Walter MacMurrough Kavanagh. Then it was on to New Ross and Fethard for other confirmations which led him naturally to the Palace, Waterford where he dined and slept. The following day he preached at the choral festival there and then motored home.

Later in the month two more ordination candidates arrived to stay at the Palace for their examination. He ordained them in the cathedral on Trinity Sunday: "Ridgeway preached a good sermon". The following day was typical of the energetic way in which he operated: he left Kilkenny at 8, spoke with the rector at Maryborough, then took a train to Birr where he was collected by a Colonel Newbold who drove him to Seirkieran, Co. Offaly – a detached portion of Ossory diocese – where he held a small confirmation. After that, he caught the 4.50 train to Dublin where he dined at the Trinity Monday feast. Various meetings then ensued in Dublin including the Representative Church Body and the Council of Alexandra College. But he was back in Kilkenny by Wednesday evening just in time to act as host to Armitage Robinson, the Dean of Wells, who stayed for a week during which he conducted a Quiet Day for 30 clergy and preached at the choral festival – "we had c.150 people to tea afterwards".

At the beginning of June he did three confirmations in Ferns diocese – Enniscorthy, Gorey, Newtownbarry – and he dined and slept with the Hall Dares at their house. They then motored him over to Carlow where he dined and slept with the Bruens at Oakpark – "dinner party of 12 in the evening". He presided at the Leighlin diocesan council at Carlow and returned to Kilkenny by train. Then he devoted time to the writing of his primary visitation charge which he proceeded to deliver on separate occasions to Leighlin diocese and Ossory diocese. In the second half of June he preached at Kilfane and lunched with the Powers, the principal parishioners, and was driven by the diocesan registrar to Ferns for his visitation there after which he left for Dublin by train for the usual Representative Church Body and Bishops' meetings. The end of the month saw him driving Canon D.F.R. Wilson to New Ross to preach at the choral festival there and attending a garden party at the Deanery in Kilkenny. In spite of all that, he managed quite a bit of golf with Colonel Herbert Bernard, Mrs Bernard's brother, who was staying with them. Then at the beginning of July he was in London staying with Sir Edward Carson and spending whole days at the British Museum. But he also found time to attend the bishops' dinner at the Mansion House and a garden party at Lambeth Palace while he and Sir Edward had lunch with the Marquess and Marchioness of Londonderry. Then he moved to stay with the Harmsworths at Montaque Square; he dined with Harmsworth at the House of Commons. Then on 15 July he went to Cambridge to lecture on the *Odes of Solomon*. He dined in the provost's lodge at King's with M.R. James "a delightful evening". Then he progressed to Ely to stay with the bishop. But all good things come to an end – 19 July was spent travelling by train and boat to Rosslare and on the following day he preached in Taghmon and Horetown and then home to Kilkenny by 7.30. The following Sunday he was in Bray preaching at the jubilee of Christ Church in the morning and unveiling a tablet to Archdeacon Scott at St Paul's in the evening. But then after only 11 days in Ireland he returned to England – to Wells to stay with the dean during which he preached in the cathedral. After 13 days there he returned to Ireland – this time to the North Wall in Dublin. Then he went to Straffan to stay with the Bartons and preached morning and evening on the Sunday in Straffan church. He arrived home on 18 August and during the remainder of that month held confirmations in Knocktopher and Carlow and preached in Burnchurch, Killeshin and Mothel.

The pace of diocesan work quickened in September: he preached in Horetown, Clonmore and Bilboa, and chaired the Leighlin and Ferns synods and the Ossory council. When he got to Clonegal he found "a big party of young people at Huntington Castle". After the Ossory synod he noted "very tired" which was hardly surprising since they had 70 people to lunch. The harvest festival season now began; he preached at Gorey, Leskinfere and St Canice's Cathedral. No wonder that on 1 October he escaped to England again (after doing a wedding at Clomantagh). A main purpose of the trip seems to have been to preach for the Revd H. Monroe at East Sheen which he did morning and evening on Sunday 5 October "despite the pain of a sore throat" which persisted; obliging him to cancel all his engagements – he hid himself at the Athenaeum and eventually returned to Ireland on October 10 when he plunged into Dublin engagements – he preached on Sunday the 12th at St Matthias in the morning and Christ Church, Kingstown, in the evening and during the following week attended the Representative Church Body, a bishops' meeting and spent a day at the Record Office.

During the latter half of October he preached in Kells, Gowran and Staplestown and lunched with the principal parishioners in each case. On 30 October the Duchess of St Alban's, Lady Alice Beauclerk, the Marquess of Ormonde and Lady Constance Butler came to lunch "a cheery party".

In mid-November he went to Dublin to stay with Louis Claude Purser (senior fellow of TCD); "he had a little dinner for me at Jammet's restaurant". He preached in the college chapel on the following morning and in St Stephen's in the evening. He attended the Representative Church Body and a bishops' meeting that week and then left for England on 20 November – first he conducted a quiet day at St Peter's, Northampton, at which 50 ladies were present, and went on to Oxford, staying at Christ Church deanery where Mr Lloyd George was also staying and with whom he had "a little talk" after breakfast. He went to the university sermon on the sin of pride – "very bad" – and preached at evensong in the cathedral. Then it was back to Dublin on 24 November where he took the chair at a meeting at Alexandra College. Then home to Kilkenny where five ordination candidates arrived for dinner and subsequent examination. His last engagement for the month was "a painful interview with Murray of Clomantagh in which I had to rebuke him for his attitude to his parishioners".

In December he visited Castlecomer twice – once to conduct a confirmation and secondly to ordain two deacons there; there was, as on every month, a Representative Church Body meeting and a bishops' meeting in Dublin and on the 17th he had a joint finance committee – "10 men, 7 of them at luncheon", he noted, "very tired and very bad cold". On 22 December he and Mrs Bernard escaped to London and Paris – he attended the embassy church there on Christmas day and went to the American church on Sunday 28 December.

So ended a fairly typical year of his four years in Kilkenny – noteworthy for the fact that his social intercourse was almost exclusively with the gentry and for the number of times that he travelled to England.

All this was in many ways an idyllic existence which gave him ample opportunity to keep up his English contacts; in 1912 for example he conducted a Quiet Day for the English bishops at Lambeth. It came to an end when he became Archbishop of Dublin in 1915.

The Dublin to which he returned was quite different to the one he had left. The world war now dominated everything where the Protestant community was concerned.

In spite of this there was a heavy load of public engagements, church services and meetings to be attended, and of course he continued to find time for several trips to London each year, and for the writing of many books.

On 7 October 1915 he was chosen as Archbishop of Dublin by the house of bishops. He received stacks of telegrams and hosts of letters all of which were acknowledged in his own hand: on October 16 he wrote "letters from morning till night".[20] He was still in Kilkenny initially and having to run both bishoprics; for example on 1 October he visited both cathedrals and the Palace in Stephen's Green and then returned to Kilkenny. On 1 November he was enthroned in Christ Church; on the following day he presided at a Board of Nomination for Inch parish (Glendalough diocese) and that afternoon he was enthroned at Kildare after which he returned by train to Kilkenny. He noted in his diary "very tired", which was hardly surprising. In the same month he had to chair the three synods of Dublin, Glenadalough and Kildare plus a joint meeting of the synods on 19 November. He noted afterwards: "very tired in the evening". By Christmas the Bernards had moved to Dublin and into the Palace; he spent December 24 at "interviews and letters and unpacking at the Palace". But there was no let-up at Christmas. On Christmas Day after preaching at Christ Church he dined with the Chief Justice in the evening and on Sunday 26 December he preached in St Mary's chapel of ease in the morning and in St

Stephen's in the evening, while on 28 December he consecrated John Gregg as Bishop of Ossory. On the following day he left for England.

But he closed his diary for 1915 not with any mention of the archbishopric but with a sad reflection, "A very sad year for us all and the burial of hope so far as this world is concerned. But the lad is safe I am sure."[21] This was of course a reference to the death of his son Robert fighting at Gallipoli.

He was in England until 25 January during which he stayed at the Deanery, Wells, with Dean & Mrs Robinson and then moved to London where he gave several sittings to "Mr Neale the portrait painter". During this trip he preached at Westminster Abbey "to a great congregation" and dined with Sir Edward Carson and his wife; with the Earl[22] and Countess of Desart and also spent some time in the reading room of the British Museum. Then it was back to Dublin of course by train and boat and the hectic life inseparable from the archbishopric. His engagements in what was left of January gave some idea of what this entailed:

JAN 28   Instituted Strong in the Palace chapel as rector of Arklow. Spoke at the Classical Association annual meeting on Plato and poetry.

JAN 29   Dined at the vice-regal Lodge and took Lady Wimborne in to dinner.

JAN 30   Preached St James and dined with the provost (the Revd J.P. Mahaffy)

Naturally the 1916 Rebellion came as a bolt from the blue and a stab in the back. The archbishop had left Dublin by the 9.15 train on Easter Monday to stay with the Earl of Desart at Desart Court near Kilkenny. As he put it, "At 12 noon a riot of Sinn Feiners broke out in Dublin and many people were killed". Bernard didn't hear the news until he and Lord Desart went into Kilkenny to play golf on the Tuesday; he returned to Dublin at once on the first train for 36 hours and found all well at the Palace in Stephen's Green. In his day by day account of the rebellion as seen from the Palace he includes the fact that a bullet entered his daughter's bedroom. By Sunday the

College of Surgeons had fallen and "the Green comparatively safe". The archbishop went to service at St Ann's and gave "a little address of cheer".

The list of his engagements in 1916 showed just how demanding the archbishopric could be even without the political meetings and discussions which the Easter Rising entailed. Thus he began the week of 19 March with an ordination of deacons at Christ Church Cathedral followed by confirmations on each of the following weekdays except for 23 March but he made up for this by doing two on 24 March. Then on Sunday the 26th he preached at St Werburgh's, and did four confirmations on the following weekdays. No wonder by the Friday (having given the David Wilsons and Dean Mease lunch) he could write "very tired in the afternoon".

Of course he wasn't just archbishop of Dublin – he was also bishop of Kildare and Glendalough, which meant that Counties Kildare and most of Wicklow were also under his jurisdiction. As at Kilkenny, he tended to stay with the nobility and gentry and from there make forays into neighbouring parishes to conduct confirmations and consecrate burial grounds – often of a private nature. Thus on Monday 12 June 1916 he set off for Edenderry in Co. Offaly, one of his most distant Kildare parishes, where he held a confirmation and consecrated a private burial ground. He stayed with Mr & Mrs Palmer at Rahan that night and held a confirmation at Geashill on the following day. Then he proceeded to Mountmellick to consecrate another burial ground and stayed that night at Rynn with Mrs Croasdaile. By 14 June he had reached Coolbanagher "and interviewed discontented parishioners". He lunched at the rectory there and proceeded to Lea for a confirmation after which he stayed the night at Lea Vicarage with Chancellor Graham. On June 15 he motored to Kildare itself where he lunched at the deanery and preached at the choral festival in the cathedral. From there he proceeded to Athy to stay at Kilmorony with Lady Weldon. He did a confirmation there on the following day and also one at Dunlavin. By Saturday 17 June he was back at the Palace dealing with ordination candidates whom he would ordain at Christ Church Cathedral on the following morning. That evening he went out for a stroll with

Lord Iveagh and noted "very tired this evening" – which was not surprising.

That autumn of 1916 he preached at no less than eight harvest festivals as well as conducting a Quiet Day in Cork cathedral for about 100 clergy. October was inevitably a particularly heavy month: on the first day of the month he was still in Cork where he celebrated and preached at St Fin Barre's in the morning and preached at St Luke's in the evening. On the Monday morning he left the palace there and took a train to Portarlington where he was met by Mrs Adare's motor car which brought him to Rathdaire. He preached a harvest sermon there at 4 and another at Coolbanagher to which he was motored for 8. Then on the Tuesday he lunched at Portarlington with Canon Coll, who then motored him to Rathangan for another harvest sermon; he reached home "very tired" by the 8 o'clock train from Kildare. Then followed more harvest sermons on three successive days – the last necessitating another visit of Kildare Cathedral after which he slept at Palmerstown with the Earl and Countess of Mayo.

Then in the second half of October he had the three diocesan synods plus a joint meeting of the synods which he laconically noted as "tiring but peaceful enough". As if all this wasn't enough he insisted on holding visitations of all three dioceses – something that is not enjoined by the Constitution of the Church of Ireland.[23] The Dublin visitation in Christ Church Cathedral went on all day on 23 October; he noted in his diary "tiring – the only person who gave trouble was Le Fann".[24]

And so it went on – in addition to which there were political meetings and on many evenings either he and Mrs Bernard had people to dinner or were asked out to dinner elsewhere. Although he was heavily involved in the Irish Convention which met in 1917 and 1918, his other work was not neglected. Thus on 14 January 1918 he presided at a Board of Nomination for Carnalway (diocese of Kildare), lunched with Lady Ardilaun, and presided both at the Board of Education and at a meeting of the Royal Irish Academy.[25] On 18 January he presided at a protest meeting against further facilities for divorce, and on January 21 he presided at a Board of Patronage for Dunganstown (diocese of Glendalough) "where I was outvoted".[26] On 6 February while he was in London with a convention delegation to see Lloyd George he went to Lambeth Palace "to dine and sleep". On 15 February he unveiled a memorial tablet at Christ Church, Leeson Park and preached at a big service in Rathmines church in the evening while on 5 March he admitted a lay reader in the Palace chapel, married Major Fitzmaurice to Miss Foot at St Bartholomew's and then held a confirmation at St Matthew's, Irishtown. Since he had also attended the convention that day it is no wonder that he noted "tired" in his diary. On the following day on which the convention was adjourned because of John Redmond's death he and his wife held a luncheon at the palace at which the guests were the Duke of Abercorn, Lord & Lady Midleton, Lady Powerscourt and the Earl of Desart. That every guest held a title was an indicator of the circle in which Bernard moved.

Later that month, in addition to attending the convention every day, he held confirmations at North Strand and St George's and on 22 March unveiled a memorial to Archbishop Peacocke at Christ Church Cathedral. The pace of entertaining was unrelenting: that same day Lord Midleton, Lord Desart and Lord F. FitzGerald came to tea and the Duke of Abercorn and Erskine Childers to meet the Marquess and Marchioness of Ormonde at dinner. On 15 May he noted: "we had a small dinner party"; the guests nonetheless numbered ten! On 1 May he had eight ordination candidates at the Palace all day for examination and noted, "the state of Ireland deplorable". On 21 June he went down to Kildare for a confirmation and noted "nearly 80 soldiers besides the usual boys and girls".

In July 1918 he was in London where on 14 July he preached to two dozen people at the Chapel Royal at 12.15 and in Westminster Abbey to 2,000 people at 6.30 – after which he had supper at the deanery. On 20 July he spent a delightful morning on the river at Henley with Cecil Harmsworth MP and the expenses of his entire London trip came to £8.16s.4d

In September he began his autumn manoeuvres built round harvest preachments. On 12 September he left Dublin to stay at Shelton Abbey[27] near Arklow, the seat of the Earl of Wicklow. The following day represented a surprise for all concerned: "did some harvesting with Lord Wicklow as his men are on strike". While staying at Shelton Abbey he preached at Ballinatone, Macreddin and Aughrim. He then motored to Kilkenny where he had lunch with the Marquess and Marchioness of Ormonde and then moved on to Desart Court to stay with Lord Desart. From there he proceed to the deanery at Cashel and preached at a harvest festival in the cathedral after which there was a large reception at the deanery. He noted in his diary, "very tired".[28] Then he motored to Durrow to stay with Mrs Hamilton-Stubber and by 20 September he had arrived in Lucan to preach at another Harvest Festival. The following day brought something different: "a meeting of the city clergy in the chapter room at Christ Church Cathedral to consider the coal shortage and hours of service".

Throughout most of October he was based in Dublin and his diary shows both the variety of his engagements and his fulfilling of preachments in spite of not feeling well. Thus on 4 October in spite of this he was driven to Kenure where he preached a harvest sermon, had tea afterwards with Lady Palmer and came home by train. He was still unwell on Sunday the 6th when he did not get up until 12.30. On 10 October he went down to Kildare and held a visitation and he notes that the visitation dinner cost him £4.11s.0d. The following day he brought the Revd J.M. Robinson[29] before the Court of the General Synod "for contumacy and disobedience"; Robinson was censured and suspended for three months. On the next day four Baptist ministers came to see him on their way to the front. He described them as "nice men". On Sunday 13 October he preached in the morning at Christ Church Cathedral on the sinking of the Leinster and in the evening accompanied by his wife and daughter Alice he dined at the vice-regal lodge at which King Manoel of Portugal was also present. On 17 October he had both the Glendalough and Kildare synods and "a tiresome bishops meeting".

On 20 October he was in Derry where he celebrated in the cathedral at 11.30 and preached at 3.30 to a congregation of women and at 8 to a big congregation of men who included Presbyterians and

Methodists. On the following day he presided at the opening of the Sailors Rest in Buncrana and gave a lecture in the Guildhall at Derry on his visit to Russia. On 23 October he left the "hospitable deanery" on the 2.45 train for Dublin. The flavour of his Dublin life is well conveyed by his diary entry for 29 October: he was at the Record Office for most of the day; then he dined with the high sheriff at the Gresham Hotel where he sat next to Viscount French, the Lord Lieutenant – "a big dinner of 200 men with tiresome long speeches".

During most of the first half of November he was ill and unable to carry out engagements. By 14 November he was feeling better – as a result he had many interviews and he dined with Chief Justice Molony to meet the Hon. W.H. Bruce, "an educational authority", and others. There were fourteen at the dinner. On the following night he and his wife dined with the Arnotts – "a banquet of sixteen". At the end of November ordination candidates were examined over two days and this entailed a luncheon for fourteen. In December he gave "a poor lecture" on the psalms in St Ann's, Dawson Street, and presided and gave an address at a meeting of the Royal Irish Academy to welcome Lord French as visitor. Also this month a rare ecumenical gesture occurred when he attended a service at Rutland Square Presbyterian Church "as a mark of fraternal good will". On 11 December he inspected Wilson's Hospital at Multyfarnham and noted "a long tiring day", but this was something that he didn't have to do: it wasn't in his diocese, or even province.

In 1919 he continued to give time to the Anti-Partition League: on 3 January he dined with Lord Iveagh to meet Lord Midleton, Lord Desart, Lord Kenmare, Lord Oranmore and Browne and Col. Walter Guinness (all of whom were prominent in the league) and also to deal with parish problems at the micro level: Coolbanagher was still giving trouble and the principal parishioner, Lord Portarlington,[30] called to discuss the situation on January 2. The court of the General Synod took up 9 and 22 January: at the meeting on the 9th Bernard had "a passage with the Lord Chancellor – very good for him".[31]

Then on 23 January the archbishop & Mrs Bernard left for a visit to England. They stayed at Lumley Castle, "the oldest inhabited house in England", with the Dowager Marchioness of Londonderry and then proceeded to the deanery at Durham where he preached in the cathedral at the annual commemorations of benefactors – "big congregation". They then left for London by train and after a three-hour wait at Waterloo arrived at Peper Harow near Guildford, the seat of Lord Midleton. On 1 February they arrived at Dean's Yard Westminster to stay with Canon & Mrs Carnegie and at dinner there they met the American ambassador and Mrs Davis, Lord Milner, Col. Endicott & Mrs Alfred Lyttleton and others, making in all "a delightful party of 12". On the following day which was a Sunday, he preached in St Margaret's Westminster at 11 and attended evensong at the abbey. At tea afterwards in the deanery they met HRH, the Duchess of Albany,

They left "hospitable Dean's Yard" on 5 February and moved to 28 Montague Square to stay with the Cecil Harmsworths. On the following day they lunched with the Marquess and Marchioness of Londonderry and also there were Lord Farquhar, Winston Churchill and "some soldiers". That evening they went to Lambeth Palace for two nights. While there Bernard had a talk with Archbishop Randall Davidson about his own affairs. After that it was Eton College to stay with the provost, Montague James. He preached in the chapel there and dined in hall. Then they went home on 11 February "after a pleasant outing".[32]

On 1 April he conducted a Quiet Day for 30 clergy in Limerick Cathedral; he stayed with the bishop and had tea with the dean. April 3 and 4 were typical of many days in that they were devoted to letters and interviews while on 16 April the Lord Chancellor called "about the Clonmel synod".[33] Easter Monday too was devoted to "many letters". On 26 April prior to the institution of a new rector of Coolock, there were "many – too many – interviews".

At the end of April he made a pleasant visit to stay with the Earl and Countess of Donoughmore at Knocklofty,[34] ostensibly to preside at a meeting of the diocesan synod to elect a new bishop which was meeting at nearby Clonmel. He had a game of golf at Knocklofty "after a tiring day" and the following day was spent mostly on the river Suir watching the salmon fishers. But this time of relaxation didn't last long: he left Knocklofty for London and travelled overnight to Paddington via Rosslare. He went straight to 52 Portland Place, "Lady St Helier's hospitable house",[35] and then plunged into a whirl of dinner parties over the next nine days. Probably the main reason for his visit was the Royal Academy Banquet, "a very interesting and delightful occasion". On the Sunday he went with Ceil Harmsworth to the Temple Church and "heard a political discourse from Barnes the master". He was in the chair at a dinner of Grillions Club; also there were Lord Finlay, Lord Selborne, Lord Crawford and Lord Balfour. He dined as Lord Midleton's guest at the Broderers Company, of which he was master. Thomas Hardy the novelist and his wife dined at Portland Place to meet him. He arrived back in Dublin on 9 May: "Maudie and my 3 grandaughters were at the Palace to welcome me". The day after he arrived home reality broke in when three fellows from TCD came to see him about the provostship. Nonetheless he replied to innumerable letters which had accumulated in his absence and spoke against the admission of women in the General Synod. Then eight ordination candidates arrived at the Palace to be examined and entertained. May 21 saw two engagements which were typical of many: he presided at a board of nomination for St Kevin's parish and spoke at a parish meeting in Clontarf to welcome returned soldiers.

The end of May saw one of his confirmation tours in Kildare diocese – the speed of which makes one tired even to record it. After a visitation of TCD by himself as vice-chancellor and Chief Justice Molony, he went down to Celbridge for a confirmation at 4.00. There he was collected by Lady Wright, who motored him over to Coolcarrigan[36] for the night. From there Lady Wright motored him to Ballinafagh for Holy Communion (it was Ascension Day) and then back to Coolcarrigan. Then Lady Wright motored him to Edenderry for a confirmation and the dedication of a war memorial. That night he stayed at the rectory there. Then he was motored to Geashill for a confirmation after which he had lunch with Mrs Digby at Geashill Castle; then to Mountmellick for an afternoon confirmation after which he had tea with the rector and Mrs Wilson. Then Canon Cole motored him to Portarlington to dine and sleep.

The next day he consecrated a churchyard and held a confirmation at Portarlington; had lunch with Canon Cole and his wife and various clergy and came home by train arriving at the Palace at 5.45 on the Saturday. No wonder he spent all the next day resting, apart from attending St Ann's Dawson Street at 10.

Then on the Monday he was offered the provostship of Trinity College by Mr Bonar Law. The great advantage to him in accepting the provostship was not that it relieved him of public engagements but that it relieved him of confirmations and many interviews; it confined his work much more to Dublin itself and removed the necessity for him to make forays into Counties Wicklow and Kildare. Nonetheless, as we shall see, it was a difficult decision for him to resign his archbishopric and membership of the house of bishops – tiresome though on occasions he found the latter to be.

—⟨⟨⟨—

The Statesman

JOHN HENRY BERNARD owed nothing to his birth: he rose to leadership in the unionist community entirely by his own efforts, by which he occupied high office in the Church of Ireland. He emerged at the Irish Convention of 1917 as a leader of the southern unionists. As Patrick Buckland has pointed out, the importance of southern unionism is often overlooked: southern unionist willingness to accept home rule and to mediate between the British government and Sinn Féin paved the way for the treaty negotiations of 1921.[37] It is therefore interesting to plot his progress from unionism to anti-partitionism having parted company with the northern unionists on the way, and it is equally interesting to see how as Provost of Trinity College (1919-27) he related to a new independent Ireland (he would have said 'part of Ireland') which satisfied none of the ideals to which he had devoted his life.

The question in 1912 was whether all unionists were prepared to join in a covenant against the introduction of home rule which had been on the political agenda since the days of Parnell. In June of that year Bernard spoke at a great demonstration in the Albert Hall in London against the introduction of home rule; it was attended by

9,000 people including 1200 Irish delegates, 50 peers and 160 members of Parliament. The Right Hon. Walter Long MP[38] presided, and Bernard seconded the resolution, asserting the determination of all present to maintain the union unimpaired. He said that he had come to say two things: "loyalty is not a monopoly of Ulster and I have to say that we of the minority of the south are at one with our northern brethren in the wholeheartedness of our attachment to the union – the loyal south refused to be disassociated from the loyal north. Secondly I speak on behalf of the Church of Ireland which has a larger number of members than any other religious body in Ireland outside the Church of Rome. And I will remind this meeting that the Church of Ireland in full synod has reaffirmed her unwavering opposition and her grave distrust of home rule. It is most of all because we Irish loyalists resent being robbed of any fraction of our citizenship and of our share in our Imperial inheritance that we raise our voices today."[39]

However, at the end of August in that year, Bernard received a letter from the Earl of Bessborough, a leading layman in his diocese, suggesting a special service "for the purpose of praying for deliverance from home rule and for the guidance of Ulster"; this referred to the belief that the Ulster unionists did not have to obey the Imperial Parliament unless it allowed Ulster to opt out of the home rule legislation.

Bernard demurred and suggested the substitution of a collect instead. Lord Bessborough was not pleased: he said, "I do not think that any Roman Catholic could or would object to the Protestants of the south setting apart a special day for prayer for deliverance from home rule or any other plague."[40] Clearly the Bishop of Down (at that time Charles D'Arcy) had already agreed to the holding of special services on the morning of 28 September. The Archbishop of Dublin wrote to Bernard on 1 September saying that he thought it was unwise of the bishop to commit himself to this action because the services would be held immediately before a meeting in Belfast and they would thus be committed in the eyes of the general public in Ireland and Great Britain to acceptance of whatever action may be taken, i.e. a covenant to refuse submission to home rule.[41] The

Primate and the bishops of Derry, Kilmore and Clogher were much put out by the Bishop of Down's action. They had all agreed special prayers about the whole matter of home rule on the previous Sunday the 23rd and thus as far as possible to avoid identifying the church generally with the proceedings of the meeting on 28 September. The archbishop asked, "Should we have special prayers on the 22 September throughout the southern province as Lord Bessborough has suggested?" The archbishop's own view was to avoid in any way identifying the church with any league or covenant: "We have to consider the position of clergy and people outside Ulster if the Ancient Order of Hibernians and the land leaguers in revenge for the Belfast movement were to raise a hostility against them throughout the three other provinces." The archbishop continued: "the Ulster bishops are to issue a pastoral next Thursday; we will then know exactly what they are about to do and we may have to issue a separate pastoral. As regards prayers we might have one or two introduced into the ordinary Sunday service of a general nature", and he concludes by saying that he is writing only to the Bishops of Ossory and Cork for advice. The Archbishop of Dublin wrote again on 5 September, saying that he was relieved that the Bishop of Ossory did not like the idea of a pastoral and the Bishop of Cork was also against it, and he went on: "the great majority of the laity in the south would strongly object to being in any way identified with the Ulster movement".[42] The three bishops then settled for special prayers in the normal services on 22 September in the southern province. The Archbishop of Dublin wrote again to the Bishop of Ossory on 13 September, saying: "All the bishops are glad that we are not taking action that would bring us into line with the Ulster movement meeting on the 28th."[43]

It so happened that, at the end of September, Bernard was in North Antrim staying with Lord Macnaughton at Runcurry. He noted in his diary for 28 September: "Lucy went for service for 'Ulster Day' in Dunluce Parish Church", but he himself prudently stayed at home and on the following day (a Sunday) he contented himself with attending an 8.30 a.m. celebration.[44] But Bernard remained a unionist: when in London he stayed with Sir Edward

Carson,[45] MP for Dublin University and leader of the Irish Unionists in the House of Commons in both 1913 and 1914.[46]

War broke out in 1914 and Bernard's address to the Ossory Synod in September 1915 excited much interest. He praised all the Irish Regiments "who have died in the same trenches for us and each other ... Don't forget that the first Irish chaplain to be killed was the Roman catholic chaplain of the Dublin Fusiliers. These things ought to soften the bitterness of political antagonisms by and by ... It is unthinkable that Irishmen should draw sword on Irishmen because of political differences after the war is over."[47] The *Dundalk Democrat* waxed lyrical about it: "The address delivered by the Protestant Bishop of Ossory has attracted widespread and deserved attention because of the tolerant and patriotic spirit in which the speaker refers to the proposals, now dormant, which the country must face again after the war. We are very glad to notice that the *Irish Times* the organ of moderate responsible Irish unionists, fully endorses Dr Bernard's plea for national unity and the abandonment of the incitements to violence to which leaders of the Ulster covenant movement committed themselves two or three years ago."[48]

This drift towards an inclusive nationalism was continued by Bernard in his sermon in St Patrick's Cathedral, Dublin, on St Patrick's Day 1916. On 21 December he had received an interesting letter from the rector of Bushmills which said that he had been speaking to a local Roman catholic nationalist politician and he said that all the leaders seemed to be greatly impressed by Bernard's speech on the war and Ireland: "Mr Devlin said you're certainly not a time server seeing you made the speech when the Dublin election was imminent and he believed the nationalists would be willing to admit the difficult question of the Irish difficulty to his judgement." The rector of Bushmills went on to say: "Independence like yours is refreshing. I am both a covenanter and a unionist."[49]

Bernard had this to say in his sermon: "There was a great deal that they should do well to forget on the one side and on the other ... God alone knows what the future has in store for us ... a new social order is being evolved before our eyes. In what spirit shall we prepare to meet the coming day? Their declarations make it clearer than ever that the Ulster trouble on both sides is the work of those self-seeking politicians and that on both sides the longing for some happy national accommodation pervades what Mr Dillon would call 'the overwhelming majority' of the Irish people. Not more than a dozen politicians, all told, stand between our nation and her liberties."[50] The *Evening Herald* commented on 18 March 1916 "on a remarkable plea for tolerance and brotherly feeling between Irishmen were made yesterday by Most Revd Dr MacRory[51] in Belfast and by the Most Revd Dr Bernard in Dublin".[52]

But the rebellion in Dublin that Easter changed all that.

Many Irishmen, both unionist and Redmondite nationalists, regarded the rising as a stab-in-the-back while all eyes were fixed on the progress of the great war, in which Bernard had already lost a son fighting with the Dublin Fusiliers at Gallipoli. Bernard's reaction was characteristically severe. On 3 May *The Times* published a letter from him which caused great offence: in it he said, "this is not the time for pardoning, it is the time for punishment". In his sermon in the chapel of the Female Orphan House in Dublin on 7 May 1916 Bernard set forth his views more fully: "our hearts are full of the tragedies of the last fortnight – the devastation of the city, the blood and the wounding and the tears which the mad revolt has brought. And our uppermost thoughts are those of sadness and shame. And we are sad too when we think of the wretched men who have lost their lives trying to stir up a revolt which could never have succeeded. We are sorry, for they are and were our countrymen, wanton and wicked as their treason was. It is shameful to think that the gallant Dublin Fusiliers should have been attacked by men of their own city and too many of them killed. The good name of Dublin and of Ireland has been besmirched ... This is a greater quarrel than any between Roman catholic and Protestant, unionist and nationalist, it is the long impending quarrel between the forces of authority and the forces of anarchy."[53]

He didn't only speak in public; he also wrote to persons of authority in London and on 11 May he had a reply from Arthur Balfour MP[54] writing from the Admiralty as follows: "the degree of severity or clemency which ought to be shown in cases of rebellion such as that which has recently disgraced Dublin is difficult to determine but I do not think you need fear that the present government has the least idea of relaxing the sentences finally fixed by General Maxwell. The penalties on which he has resolved have been and will be fully carried out."[55]

Bernard had in fact plenty of opportunities to make his views known to those in government both in Ireland and in England: on May 12 he dined at the Vice-Regal Lodge to meet the prime minister, Mr Asquith "with whom I had a long talk";[56] while on 23 May General Sir John Maxwell, the Commander-in-Chief, dined at the Palace on St Stephen's Green. In that same week Mr Justice Shearman called on behalf of Lord Hardinge's commission to get any information he could give "about the causes of the Irish rebellion at Eastertide".[57] On 26 June the report of the Hardinge Commission was published. It heard evidence from 29 witnesses, and its conclusion was that "the main causes of the rebellion appear to be that lawlessness was allowed to grow up unchecked and that Ireland for several years past has been administered on the principle that it was safe and more expedient to leave the law in abeyance if collision with any faction of the Irish people could thereby be avoided."[58] In June 1916 the government lead by Lloyd George had attempted to settle the Irish question by bringing in home rule and excluding six of the Ulster counties from its operation. The executive committee of the Irish Unionist Alliance in which Bernard was a leading light was having none of this. It renewed its solemn protest against the proposed settlement of the Irish question and with sad prescience it declared:

1. The policy of endeavouring to placate American opinion, real or exaggerated, by the sacrifice of our own loyal subjects is unworthy of the British Empire and foredoomed to failure.
2. The proposed settlement is a flagrant breach of the parliamentary truce.
3. It is a concession to the recent rebellion and will be regarded by lawless men in every country as an encouragement to violence and crime.

4. It involves the partition of Ireland; a country in itself all too small as a political and economic unit.
5. Because no party in the country really desires it or welcomes its advent.
6. Because it entails the abandonment of unionist by unionists and nationalist by nationalists.
7. Because coming as it does between the recent rebellion and the Imperial conference promised by the prime minister at the end of the war, it has no possibility of success ...

On 3 June 1916 Bernard had written a letter to Mr Lloyd George which, among other things, argued that the whole of Ulster should be excluded from the operation of home rule. He said that he was as fully convinced as ever that separatist legislation for Ireland would injure Ireland's highest interest. Neither prosperity nor peace could be expected as its issue ... The concession of an independent parliament as a direct issue of the recent rebellion would be a direct incentive to lawlessness in the future on the part of the discontented. He admitted that though the proposed legislation would be bad for Ireland it was the duty of every good citizen to try to make it work smoothly if it was forced on the people. He believed that the attitude of many unionists in the south of Ireland was that they were ready to make great sacrifices to ensure any stable form of government under which life and property would be secured. "During the last six or seven years we have had only a travesty of government. The Irish people have been taught that crime (small or great) may expect to escape punishment if only it can assume a political complexion. The real need of Ireland is *government* ... and this is a thing which the young Irishmen of the present generation are quite unfamiliar with. If Ulster is excluded there will be large financial problems. The British taxpayer will have to provide heavy subsidies. But I hope that the division will be of the whole province of Ulster because:

1. It is importance that the line of division should not precisely correspond with ecclesiastical or religious differences. It will soften the asperities of north and south afterwards if the demar-

cation is made on geographical rather than on theological lines.

2. A large Roman catholic and nationalist minority will be left there. The presence of considerable minorities in both sections of Ireland will be a guarantee of fair dealing all round and it may have the ultimate consequence that north and south will come together."

He went on to argue for special treatment of southern unionists in the Dublin parliament (in the House of Commons as well as in the Senate).[59]

But we know that this view was not shared by Lloyd George. On 24 July Lloyd George gave a public assurance that under no conditions would the six counties be forced into a home rule government against their will.[60]

On 16 September Bernard had an opportunity to inform King George V and Queen Mary about the Irish situation at first hand. He dined that evening at Windsor Castle and took Queen Mary into dinner – "had much talk about Ireland with her and afterwards with his majesty".[61] On 25 September he dined again at the Vice-Regal Lodge and "had a long talk with Lord Wimborne as I was trying to persuade him of the need for compulsory service in Ireland", while on the 27th he called to see Sir John Maxwell about the state of Ireland.[62]

The archbishop set out his views at some length in an article in the October issue of the *National Review*. He argued that home rule was now on the statute book and that it was improbable that it would be repealed. He presumed that members of the government, who were formerly unionists, still believed that separate legislation for Ireland was inconsistent with the highest interest of England and Ireland. That was his own conviction. The six north-eastern counties had been promised by the government that they would not be forced to accept home rule and that the home rule act would be amended before it was put into force ... and he said, "the exclusion of Ulster is intensely unpopular in Ireland as a whole and so we have come to an impasse".

The archbishop went on: "the dreamers who look for an Irish

Republic resent the union with Great Britain ... the plain fact is that Ireland can never be allowed to become independent of the sister country – the rebellion of last April demonstrated this – the words engraved on the Parnell monument in Dublin 'No man has the right to fix the boundary to the march of a nation' is a foolish sentence. I hope with all my heart that Irishmen will try to reach a settlement among themselves which may tend to the prosperity of our country and the strengthening of our national character. I am quite sure that those who used to be unionists are ready to make great sacrifices in their endeavour to make friends with their nationalist fellow countrymen. There must be 'give and take' and the concessions should be on both sides. But the first principle is that Ireland is and will remain part of the empire. The great majority of Irishmen whatever be their political profession know in their hearts that Ireland cannot be totally separated from England, but, as is generally the case, the irreconcilable minority exercises an influence out of all proportion to its number. Moral courage is a quality rare in Ireland."

He considered that the main cause of the increasing popularity of Sinn Féin was the fact that some leaders of the recent rebellion were executed. "No Irish nationalist expects to be punished for political crimes no matter how grave may be the consequences. The report of the Hardinge commission makes plain that under Mr Birrell and Lord Aberdeen the first principle of government was held to be that there should be *no* government. Only fifteen rebels were executed in all, although hundreds of lives of soldiers and citizens alike were sacrificed in that mad and wicked enterprise. Sir John Maxwell acted with great moderation as well as good judgement, but it was enough that anyone should be executed for treason to provoke a very angry feeling throughout the country which had been educated to believe that treason was no more than a political eccentricity and that the killing of soldiers and policemen was not murder. But the future great quarrel will be between the forces of authority on one side and the forces of disorder and anarchy on the other. It is of comparatively little importance in Ireland what political badge is assumed by the government provided that it *governs*.

Much depends on the line taken in the near future by the Roman Catholic priesthood – in many cases the younger Roman catholic priests favour the rebellion of Easter week. Whenever advocates in high places declare themselves on the side of law and order – they will find hearty support from the loyalists of the south and the west – the only class which has not resorted to arms in support of its political opinions in the years 1913–1916 ...... they abhor the idea of a civil war. I have no scheme of compromise to offer, no one believes that the particular scheme of home rule now on the statute books can be worked without Ulster. There is an irreconcilable difference between those who think that Ireland can be wholly divorced from England and those who think that they must always remain in close alliance and that their foreign policies, their army and their navy must be identical. It is of the last importance, that if there is to be fighting in Ireland after the war is over, Irishmen should not be allowed to fight with Irishmen ... it is the duty of parliament to see that its authority is maintained by the armed forces of the Crown; that is the meaning of government. It would be the crime of crimes for parliament to pass a controversial measure and then to allow Irishmen to 'fight it out' as if it were only a private matter."

What was the reaction in Ireland to this article? One reaction came from Walter MacMurrough Kavanagh, a leading layman in Leighlin diocese, who was unusual in being of indisputable Irish descent and also in being a nationalist landlord. He wrote to the archbishop on 9 October 1916 about his article in the *National Review*: "Of course you speak at a time when we nationalists (of the type that I am) have no right to answer back ... We are down in the depths but I must say that we have been treated quite fairly – even kindly – there is no jumping on the fallen foe. As to 'independence', the majority of us nationalists do not ask for it. But all the same you must not take away from us our dreams or our ideals."[63] A rather different correspondent was Dr Kelly, the Roman catholic Bishop of Ross, who wrote on 20 November 1916: "I am delighted with your Grace's article. It is wise and courageous. Only an extremist can take offence. Of course you are too impartial as between Ulster and Dublin rebels!"[64]

On 24 November 1916 the archbishop commented to Lord Wimborne, the viceroy, on a set of proposals produced by the government for Ireland. He said that the four points of the government's proposals were:

1. Home rule immediately for all of Ireland.
2. Protestants and Roman Catholics to have equal representation in an Irish parliament.
3. Imperial supremacy and control of military and naval bases.
4. Compulsory military service to be immediately required in all of Ireland.

He informed the viceroy that he had discussed these conditions widely and that the scheme did not meet with much favour: "Ulster won't look at it – for them 'home rule is Rome rule'. Compulsory service will be resisted by all schools of nationalists." The archbishop didn't think that the present government would stick to imperial supremacy and conscription when the opposition started. Asquith would yield as he did with the Sinn Féin rebellion. Bernard thought conscription was necessary to win the war but that it could not come without bloodshed, and he told the viceroy that the sacrifice of 500–1,000 lives in Ireland was worth it if the war could be shortened by a single day. Sooner or later the threatened insurrection would come in Ireland. "It is better that it comes at once. I need hardly add that the policy of sending back to Ireland, unpunished, numbers of men who took part in the recent rebellion will be interpreted as the outcome of fear and not of generosity on the part of the government." The government should compel Ireland to take her share of responsibility in this hour of imperial danger.[65] On 6 December Asquith resigned as prime minister. Bernard described this as "a good thing" – and he was succeeded by Lloyd George.

On 21 March 1917 Bernard suggested in a letter to The Times the gathering which finally became known as the Irish Convention of 1917/18. In his letter he recognised that some measure of self-government for Ireland would be recommended to Parliament, and Ulster was going to be allowed to stay out: "partition is hateful to

Irishmen but if it is to come it is desirable that its detail should be considered by those who know Ireland"; and then he went on to suggest a conference of Irish political leaders and other representatives of Irish public opinion: "I desire peace and goodwill in Ireland and I believe that this may even yet come if Unionists will agree to discuss schemes of self-government while nationalists agree to repudiate the fanatics who dream of an independent Irish rebellion." On 13 June 1917 Lloyd George wrote to him duly inviting him to be a member of a "convention of Irishmen of all parties for the purpose of producing a scheme of Irish self-government".[66]

But first, in May 1917, Bernard received from the Roman catholic Bishop of Derry a request to sign an appeal on the subject of partition "having read in the public press on more than one occasion your patriotic pronouncements in regard to Irish affairs"; and he informed him that a number of Catholic bishops and some Protestant bishops had agreed to sign. This letter is endorsed by Bernard: "I refused".[67] The Bishops of Ossory, Tuam and Killaloe did sign. This appeal caused something of a flurry in the Irish episcopate of which Bernard was obviously an important member. Later in May he received a letter from the Primate enclosing a letter which the Primate had sent to the Bishop of Ossory (Dr John Gregg) as follows: "the joint action of three bishops of the Church of Ireland with the Roman hierarchy compelled the Ulster bishops to take some public action, as I hear incalculable injury is being done to the Church in the north, but before issuing our statement I should like as a matter of loyalty to our brethren to have a full meeting of bishops." In his covering note to the Archbishop of Dublin he said, "I fear, my dear archbishop, that much injury has been done by this political move of the three bishops."[68] This matter was discussed at a meeting of the bishops and they ensured that no resolution should appear before the General Synod on the subject of home rule. The *Irish Times* commented: "no doubt this was a wise decision, for the advertisement of inevitable differences of opinion between the northern and the southern clergy about the exclusion of Ulster might have created a misleading impression in the country".[69]

The Irish Convention finally met on 25 July 1917 in the Regent

House in Trinity College and Bernard's role in it was to be an important one both for him and for the southern unionists whose views he represented. As Patrick Buckland has pointed out, after 1916 once the immediate crisis was past, some southern unionists including Bernard, began to consider plans for a settlement of the Irish question on lines other than those laid down by the Home Rule Act.[70] Moreover they resented the Ulster unionists' decision to accept partition, because partition would make home rule even less tolerable to the southern minority by depriving it of the support of the compact unionist group in the north-east.

The convention consisted of some 95 members and the largest group (35) were appointed by the local authorities. The government appointed fifteen members of whom four were peers and three were holders of academic posts. Sinn Féin boycotted the convention: their views being represented by Edward MacLysaght. The Roman catholic hierarchy was represented by four bishops and that of the Church of Ireland by the Archbishops of Armagh and Dublin. The Presbyterian Moderator was also a member. The Ulster unionists had five representatives, as had the southern unionists. The leader of the southern unionists was an interesting figure – Lord Midleton, who, although he drew rents from in and around Midleton in Co. Cork, had no Irish residence. In England he had held three junior ministerial posts and had been secretary of state for both war and India. But he had been elected chairman of the Irish Unionist alliance in 1909 and he had led the fight against home rule ever since then. The Irish parliamentary party also had five representatives, including Redmond and Devlin, but not including Dillon. It was reckoned that those of nationalist sympathy comprised just over half of the convention membership.

But before examining his role in the convention it is as well to note that both in the convention and socially he allied himself entirely with the Irish peerage, of which he seemed to think he was an honorary member. Thus he actually moved across St Stephen's Green to stay at Iveagh House with Lord Iveagh while the convention was sitting in Dublin. The other members of the house party were the Duke of Abercorn, Viscount Midleton, the Marquess of

Londonderry, the Earl of Desart, the Earl of Mayo, Lord Oranmore and Browne and Colonel Addison. He notes that on one evening at Iveagh House during the convention there were sixteen to dinner. When it moved to Belfast he stayed at Mount Stewart with the Marquess of Londonderry (a northern unionist member of the convention) and in Cork he stayed at Castle Bernard, the seat of the Earl of Bandon which had been lent to Lord and Lady Midleton while the convention was sitting in Cork. On many weekends he and Mrs Bernard were the guests of Irish peers including Granard and Fingall who were actually Roman catholics. In contrast the Primate (Dr J.B. Crozier) endeavoured to maintain his independence in the convention with such success that after six weeks the Ulster group was said to be getting uneasy and suspicious about him;[71] whereas Bernard identified himself entirely with the southern unionists and the southern peers in particular.

The choice of Sir Horace Plunkett as chairman was a great and probably fatal mistake. The father of the co-operative movement in Ireland, he had been elected as a unionist MP for South County Dublin in 1892. But he talked too much and believed that men of goodwill could always by rational discussion reach agreement. He wasted the convention's time and patience by insisting on a series of debates at the beginning of the convention work. As early as 17 October 1917 Lord Midleton had obviously lost all patience with him. Writing to Bernard "from the train", he said: "Yesterday we had a most futile meeting – nearly three hours of "Plunkettiana". It was a face-saving business ... I am afraid Plunkett is a spent force if he ever was one at all – the Ulster members are furious with him."[72] Another problem militating against the success of the convention was the hopelessly unrealistic attitude being displayed by the Irish government. In the same letter to Bernard, Lord Midleton described a conversation which he had had with Lord Wimborne, the Lord Lieutenant: "I had a long confidential talk with Wimborne last night at his wish and I told him what we all feel. He counters that the policy of no open breach with Sinn Féin, otherwise regrettable, must be kept up until all hope of the convention agreeing to something is gone. He told me that Redmond on Friday was still most sanguine of a settlement. I doubt if they fully realise the abyss which is opening ..., unless Redmond and company will now take responsibility on the right side, they must go under."

The main hope for the convention was that the southern unionists and the nationalists would agree on some scheme. At the beginning of January it seemed as if a large majority of the convention might agree on a settlement along lines laid down by Midleton and Redmond, but then Plunkett put off the crucial vote and turned the convention instead to consider a scheme of land purchase.[73]

What was Bernard's role in all this? In August he was elected to the standing committee of twenty and on the 22nd he lunched with Sir William Goulding to meet Joseph Devlin MP. On 28 August he notes in his diary that Lord Midleton made an important speech and "Lysaght the Sinn Féiner an impudent one".[74] That evening he dined at the Vice-regal Lodge. It was a "well ordered and hospitable convention party". On the following day he made a speech "which was thought to be good. Redmond told me that he was going to answer it and that I had raised the really important issues".[75] In his speech he had said that any scheme must have (1) a reasonable prospect of prosperity for Ireland, (2) a security for the interests of the empire especially in time of war, and (3) a security that the interest shall not be ignored of the only section of Irishmen who have always obeyed the lay and who intend to do so in future.[76] The southern unionists as a whole had played a relatively small part in the convention prior to November 1917. But then they began to intervene energetically: they were desperately anxious to secure a compromise which would go some way towards satisfying national aspirations, maintain the connection between Ireland and Great Britian, preserve the unity of Ireland and protect minorities. Midleton and Bernard, the leaders of southern unionism, believed that by a well-timed display of authoritative commonsense they could decisively influence the convention's proceedings.[77]

Bernard attacked the northern unionists, saying that a mere *non possumus* on the fiscal question simply would not do; as a result of this Barrie (the leader of the northern unionists) went so far as to admit that an Irish parliament must have some taxing powers. Then

Midleton "took the plunge" and produced his compromise proposals. Under them an Irish parliament would have control of internal taxation (including excise duties) but custom duties would remain under the control of the imperial parliament.

On 5 December 1917 Midleton and Bernard had an interview with Lloyd George at 10 Downing Street. They emphasised that Ulster stood in the way of any settlement: if pressed, the northern unionists might be willing to acquiesce in a settlement which granted them administrative autonomy. Bernard pointed out that the only way of moving Ulster from its *non possumus* attitude was by suggesting that she would probably fare worse in the future when the next parliament was in being. Lloyd George described the southern unionist memorandum as "statesmanlike" but he did not say that Ulster would be forced to accept a settlement. Bernard stressed perceptively the growing danger from Sinn Féin and the determination of the southern unionists never to agree to the division of Ireland: could he have known that within five years Sinn Féin would be triumphant, and partition an established fact? The archbishop noted: "a disappointing conclusion and it points to the break-up of the convention".[78]

But the convention did not break-up: at least not yet. It met on 2 January 1918 and began a three-day debate on Midleton's proposals. Speaking on the last day of the debate, Redmond emphasised the sacrifices made both by the northern unionists and the southern unionists and attacked the Ulster delegates as being pledge-bound to consult an outside body and for refusing to "give-an-inch". Very significantly, that afternoon he tabled an amendment asking the convention to agree to Midleton's proposals provided that they were adopted by the government as a settlement of the Irish question and legislative effect given to them at once.

At this point it seemed as if a large majority of the convention might have agreed on this settlement, supported as it was both by Midleton and Redmond, but, as we have seen, Sir Horace Plunkett fatally failed to secure a decision. Things could only go down-hill from that high peak, as it gave time to extremists on both sides to press their views on members of the convention.

The next significant event was an interview which Lord Midleton, the archbishop and Lord Desart had with the prime minister, Lord Curzon and Bonar Law on 6 February 1918. Midleton explained that his proposals which had seemed likely to receive the assent of a large majority of the convention on 1 January were now less favourably viewed because (1) the nationalists now felt that the U.S. demands for an Irish settlement were so strong that anything would be conceded by parliament to placate American opinion, (2) the split in the nationalist party had affected Redmond's nerves, and (3) Ulster refused to accept anything.

The prime minister asked, "Can you really coerce Ulster?" Bernard asked if the Ulster delegates had gone into the convention fortified by a special pledge that no legislation of which they disapproved would be enacted. The prime minister said "No" but what had been promised was immediate legislation if approved by a substantial majority. If Ulster unionists stood out, it would be difficult to describe the residual majority as *substantial*. The prime minister said Ulster had three fears if a Dublin parliament was established: (1) the liquor traffic, (2) education and (3) legislation re factories and industries. Maybe if two grand committees in the Irish parliament – one for Ulster and one for the rest – were set-up this might meet the difficulty. Midleton and Bernard saw no objection but said, "the one thing that all Ireland (outside Belfast) would not allow was the partition of Ulster". The prime minister concurred warmly in the view that partition was impossible. Midleton urged that Ulster should be pressed to say definitely on what conditions she needed to come into an Irish parliament. Desart said any undue deference to Ulster views would shatter the convention from the nationalist side.[79]

The convention sent a delegation to meet the prime minister at 10 Downing Street on 13 February 1918.

The prime minister appealed for yet another effect to reach agreement saying:

1. You cannot legislate as freely in war as in peace. The fiscal question and control of police must stay put for the duration of the war.
2. A settlement was only possible if partition were excluded. The

prime minister regretted personally the rejection of the partition proposals of 1916 – if accepted the unity of Ireland would soon have been achieved. But the experiment was rejected by the southern unionists as well as by the nationalists. It would be idle to propose partition again.

3. Safeguards must be provided for the vital interests of Ulster – labour must be protected against the peasant.
   He would argue for an Ulster committee in the Irish parliament with powers to veto.

4. During the war it would be impossible to break up fiscal unity of the United Kingdom, but short of full dominion powers, anything asked will be given to Ireland.[80]

To return to Ireland outside the convention: while the Ulster unionists continued to be united and immovable, a split developed in the southern unionists. At a meeting of the standing committee of the General Synod in January 1918 the Primate brought up the subject of the convention and Bernard was strongly attacked by Richard Bagwell of Marlfield, Clonmel, a landlord and a distinguished historian. He said that the archbishop was now a home ruler as the scheme which he supported was not a compromise but a surrender; while the Bishop of Down (Dr d'Arcy) expressed the Ulster unionist point of view. In February 1918 opposition to Midleton among the southern unionists became organised, and the disaffected set up the Southern Unionist Committee on 20 February 1918. They felt that their only hope lay in a continuation of the union and that with Sinn Féin in the ascendant they could expect short shift from it in any Irish parliament that might be set up.[81]

John Redmond died on 6 March 1918 and with him died any real future for the nationalist party, much less the prospect of it joining hands with the southern unionists. By the beginning of April it was time for the convention to come to an end. The nationalists and the southern unionists, by mutually making concessions, had managed to agree on a complete scheme of self-government for Ireland, but the northern unionists had stood apart from all this, and the government was not prepared to force them to come to a settlement. On 21

September 1918 all the unionist members of the convention wrote to the prime minister a letter which had been drafted at the Palace, Dublin, by Lord Midleton, Lord Desart and Archbishop Bernard:

"The release of Sinn Fein prisoners just before the meeting of the convention was followed by a great increase of republican activity throughout Ireland – they publicly defy the law of the land. It is difficult for us to consider seriously a great extension of popular liberties in the midst of such disorders and we urge that the leaders should be at once arrested and that sentences duly given should be rigidly carried out.

Without some public assurance we are convinced that Ireland will drift into a condition from which no efforts of the convention will be able to extricate her."[82]

Lord Midleton had already written a very perceptive letter to Bernard on 31 August 1918. In it he said: "I am perplexed and distressed by the whole position in Ireland. To condense it an election looms nearer every day. Labour will gain largely in England and will insist on home rule in some form unless there is a complete revulsion of feeling against Ireland. Sinn Fein will dominate the Irish electorate and one of two things may happen: the government may go back on all the pledges (satisfying Carson) to save the six counties and cut their loss for the remainder or they may possibly put aside the whole thing as so often they have done before. It is difficult to see which and I have not an idea whether our people will be wise enough to keep their powder dry and keep the alliance together."[83] But, as we know, the unionists did not keep the alliance together; Ireland was allowed to drift, and the general election at the end of 1918 swept most of the constitutional nationalists away: only six were elected as opposed to seventy-three for Sinn Fein and the southern unionists won only three seats. Soon after the election, the southern unionists finally split into two parts, and Midleton, Bernard, Jameson, Stewart and Iveagh withdrew from the Irish Unionist Alliance to form the Unionist Anti-Partition League: in the event of opposition to home rule proving futile, it would strive for safeguards for the unionists of the south and west.

In spite of their foreboding as to the effects that would follow if two parliaments were imposed on Ireland, the southern unionists of the Anti-Partition League took an active part in post-war recon-struction and were inspired by a vision of a united and prosperous Ireland.[84] Their policy was spelt out in the *Irish Times* of 15 March 1919: "the Ulster Unionist party has decided to oppose the bill which applies proportional representation to local elections in Ireland. The Irish Unionist Parliamentary Construction Committee which is closely associated with the Irish Unionist Alliance has decided to support the bill. Southern unionists want proportional representa-tion because it will safeguard the position of minorities. Northern unionists rejected it because if partition comes they want the excluded counties to be in every way a homogeneous part of Great Britain. They are preparing for partition.

"Viscount Midleton was chairman at yesterday's meeting of the Unionist Anti-Partition League – the government is pledged to a measure of partition – Unionist Ulster intends to accept exclusion. To southern unionists in this desperate emergency the League offers a policy not a helpless surrender but of aggressive and defensive action. The League argues for the transfer of initiatives from the departments in London to the Irish government, e.g. a separate ministry of health."[85]

Meanwhile the cabinet in London had begun work on what became the Government of Ireland Act 1920. It was clear that a home rule bill could no longer be postponed. As late as December 1919 the cabinet was proposing only a single Irish parliament with north-east Ireland excluded from its operations, but the bill as published provided for two political entities: northern Ireland and southern Ireland each with its own parliament. In spite of all the undertakings which he had given on the subject of partition, a division of Ireland with two parliaments was what Lloyd George now proposed. Ulster had been promised in 1914 that home rule would not be forced on it, but there was nothing about a separate parliament for northern Ireland, and when in the committee on the bill Lord Robert Cecil proposed that a parliament should not be established for northern Ireland, the northern unionists supported him with logical consistency. But they did not expect his amendment to be carried, and clearly a local parliament had its advantages for them. As Sir James Craig was to put it, it would be "a protestant parliament for a protestant people".

The parting of the ways between the northern and southern unionists had been spelled out in a letter which Bernard wrote to A.W. Samuels MP on 18 November 1918 on the eve of the general election. He said that the Ulster Protestants had completely committed themselves to accept a partition of Ireland – something which was totally opposed by the southern unionists – and he objected to Sir Edward Carson taking this line while MP for Dublin University. "He is a very old and very dear friend of mine. I recognise the difficulty of his position but it has been apparent to everyone since he agreed to partition in 1916."[86]

On 18 September 1919 Walter Long MP wrote a memorandum for the cabinet based on his recent trip to Ireland. He warned the government that it would probably be compelled to impose martial law "so as to convict the guilty and protect the innocent". He considered that Sinn Féin could be "knocked out" but that the government's policy must be severe or even ruthless.[87] He argued for a federal structure, that is, a separate parliament for northern Ireland and if the rest wouldn't accept a parliament then it should be treated as a Crown colony with direct rule.

Bernard had been sent a copy, and in his reply on 25 September 1919 he showed how his thinking had developed since the end of the convention in the previous year: "Yours is an accurate statement of present state and temper of Ireland. Neither life nor property is secure and intimidation that is practised throughout the south and north of the county is more open and violent than it has been in my life-long experience. The measures taken by the Irish government are not a whit too strong. They are necessary and the action of the Lord Lieutenant and Chief Secretary is wise as well as courageous. I regret the absence of both at the present time. No progress will be made until Asquithite newspapers as well as the Northcliffe press are ready to state with unanimity that an Irish Republic will *never* be granted by England and that the IRB deserve and must receive the sternest treatment ... You cannot pacify these extremists who have publicly averred their sympathy with bolshevism unless the absolute and complete independence of Ireland is conceded. The suggestion by a Liberal statesman last winter that de Valera should be taken into counsel by the government so as to pacify Ireland is enough to encourage the republican party to believe that if they only give enough trouble, England will in desperation cut Ireland adrift ... an Irish republic is an impossible dream ... what then is to be done?

"I agree that home rule can't be taken off statute book (though many unionists disagree with me). If we are to have home rule, as I fear (I hate to say it) is inevitable, it is far better that it should be drafted now when loyal men – loyal to the king and the empire – will have a powerful voice in defining its limitations. Speaking for myself I hope that a new home rule bill will be introduced although if there were any likelihood that home rule could be *permanently* avoided, I should prefer the traditional policy of the union." (This was the line that southern unionists took in the convention of 1917.) "Your proposal for a separate parliament for the south and the west will place the unionists of the south and west under the heel of an angry and disappointed majority. They deserve better treatment. No class in the empire behaved more loyally and less selfishly during the war. They gave all they had to give. Without bargaining as the nationalists did that home rule should be granted, or as the Ulstermen did that it should not be forced on *them*. The southern unionists are the only section of the Irish people (north or south) who have steadily obeyed the law and have refrained from threats of violence and lawlessness. It is a bad policy for England to abandon the best and most consistent friends that she has in Ireland to the oppression that they will probably have to endure if a 'federal' parliament on so-called 'democratic' principles is set up in the southern and western provinces. I confess that I am opposed to the 'partition' of Ireland. If there is to be home rule I prefer one parliament with two houses for the whole country on the lines of the majority report of the Irish Convention. If this is impossible because of Ulster I suggest that we may have to fall back on the hateful expedient of a religious franchise: providing that a certain number of seats shall be reserved for Protestants and a certain number for Roman catholics – the concurrence of both sections to be necessary for legislation for the whole island. I denounced this in the convention and I hate it but I see no way of saving loyalists and loyalism in the south and west unless (a) the Irish parliament contains a considerable number of *nominated* members or (b) by a religious franchise. But a more important question is what will be the attitude of nationalist Ireland to a federal system? I think that it will be rejected with scorn and that it will certainly be rejected unless it is made plain by all parties in the state that it represents the maximum that Britain can offer. Even then it may be rejected. In that event you propose to govern Ireland as a Crown colony. I fear that such a plan would not last two years – it would certainly be repudiated and reversed as soon as a Liberal or Labour government come into power. My own view is that if a federal system is rejected by nationalists, then the status quo should be maintained i.e. a unionist government, the Act of 1914 being repealed which nobody desires."[88]

Long replied to this on 27 September 1919. He said: "I agree with all that you say but I believe that some form of local self-government must be established not only in Ireland but throughout the United Kingdom – devolution is necessary because of the increased demands of the working classes for legislation and for reforms ... I fully share your views as to the position of the southern unionists but I am greatly puzzled as to how we are to defend them. I hate the idea of desertion and exposing them to attack but in your criticisms of my Crown colony proposal there is a failure to appreciate existing conditions. In reality, Ireland is being governed now as a Crown Colony ... The Irish government ... is as autocratic and independent of parliamentary control as if Ireland were a Crown colony."[89]

But the Government of Ireland Bill of 1920 showed how government policy was developing. In 1919 it may have been possible to believe that the union could be maintained. By 1920 it became obvious that such a hope was futile. On 19 March 1920 the Ulster unionists decided to jettison three counties of Ulster with Roman catholic majorities (Cavan, Donegal and Monaghan) and to accept a separate parliament for the remaining six counties. This decision not only cemented partition, but partition on nakedly sectarian lines. In any case, with the onset of the Anglo-Irish war the union was becoming valueless even to loyalists, for the British government was finding it increasingly difficult to maintain order. Bernard had foreseen this. When Sir Hamar Greenwood was sworn in as chief secretary at the Privy Council on 6 May 1920 he noted: "I fear Greenwood is going to play havoc with the country."[90] By 1920 a systematic campaign of murder and intimidation spread over the whole country and an Irish Republic was being established whether the British government or southern loyalists liked it or not. By January 1921 eight counties and two cities were under martial law. Throughout the south and west there was a general sense of insecurity for life and property. The British government had no defined policy for Ireland and the time for decisive action did not arrive until the treaty negotiations began in the summer of 1921.

Meanwhile the policy of the Anti-Partition League in which Bernard was a leading light was not to oppose the Government of Ireland Bill but to secure amendments which would provide safeguards for the southern unionists. Thanks to the presence of a number of southern unionist peers in the House of Lords, this policy was quite successful. They had three main objectives (1) the financial provisions were inadequate and unfair to Ireland, (2) the bill would establish the permanent partition of Ireland, and (3) the bill contained few safeguards for the unionists of the south and west despite many promises in the recent past. In particular they wanted a second chamber with considerable powers. After much debate and manoeuvring the southern unionists wrung the following safeguards from the government and of course some ministers like Long were genuinely anxious to provide them:

1. A strong senate with considerable powers over legislation.
2. Abolition of the power of the Irish parliament to impose additional income tax or surtax (the southern unionists as the richest section of the community were afraid of being financially ruined by the nationalist majority in the lower house).
3. Finality for the judicial committee of the House of Lords.

4. Protection of private property against confiscation without compensation.
5. Senate representation on the Council of Ireland which was to have increased powers particularly in respect of fisheries and animal diseases.

It should be said that these safeguards were almost identical with those suggested by the Irish Convention. Sadly for the southern unionists they were not, for the most part, reflected in the treaty of December 1921 which effectively replaced the Government of Ireland Act of 1920 and established the Irish Free State.

Bernard and his colleagues in the Anti-Partition League had been able to assist negotiations to end the union in three ways:

1. Their willingness to extend the Government of Ireland Act enabled Sinn Féin to enter into negotiations with the British government. The Anti-Partition League believed that a more generous settlement was required in Ireland and they wished to have the operation of the 1920 Act postponed.
2. They attended a conference held by de Valera in the Mansion House, Dublin as "spokeman for the Irish nation" and they were the only unionists to attend.
3. De Valera agreed there the Anti-Partition League representatives demand that the government should enter into negotiations with Sinn Féin on two conditions: that these negotiations should be direct with the British government and secondly that a truce should precede and accompany the discussions.

All this was with the Anglo-Irish war as a back-drop and it made the participation of the APL delegates all the more remarkable – no wonder that Bernard in a sermon in Westminster Abbey appealed for special prayers for those who were risking not only their lives but also their reputations.

Of course, what brought the British government to the negotiating table was not the southern unionists (no matter how useful they might be) but the success of the IRA in making the south and west of Ireland increasingly ungovernable. In a desperate attempt to uphold the government's authority, Lloyd George had let loose on Ireland a motley crew of ex-soldiers dignified by the title of the auxiliary police who have gone down in Irish folk-lore as the "Black and Tans". Despite a fearsome reputation – they burned down most of the centre of Cork as a reprisal – Bernard stoutly defended them.[91]

In spite of Bernard and others like him, a truce was called in the summer of 1921, and what life in Ireland had become for many southern unionists was well summed up by Professor E.J. Gwynn, who wrote to Bernard on 6 September 1921 as follows: "I have had a pleasant holiday thanks to the truce! This last year has made me feel for the first time that I am myself essentially English and not Irish – a man is what he inherits and what he draws in from his surroundings and for me most of us Protestants, these things are 90% English or Scottish traditions, beliefs and customs, mental furniture, all that and why I mainly fear the new order which I suppose will flood in upon us sooner or later is not so much the material loss and annoyance as the tending to cut us away from our roots, our civilisation which is bone of our bone, flesh of our flesh. I do not want myself and my children to feel aliens in their own country." That this correspondent was a professor of Old Irish and came from a famous family and was to succeed Bernard as Provost of Trinity made his letter all the more poignant. If he had been a landed loyalist in a country area of the south or west, his experiences would have been much more harrowing. A more sanguine view of developments in Ireland was put forward by the Earl of Granard; writing to Bernard from the safe distance of Forbes House in London on 1 December 1922, he said, "The Irish government seems to be going from strength to strength each day and moving more towards the right – this is all to the good".[92]

At the end of 1922 a bill to approve the constitution of the Irish Free State was introduced into the Westminster parliament. Many southern unionist peers were members of the House of Lords and the question was whether they were to move amendments to the bill or not. A meeting of a dozen Irish peers to which Bernard and the

Rt Hon. Andrew Jameson were invited was held at Lord Oranmore's London house. Lord Midleton, the President of the Anti-Partition League, wanted to increase the powers of the Senate: others did not wish to pass amendments and Jameson strongly advised against any further attempt to improve the Constitution. Lord Midleton's proposal was soundly beaten and Bernard's view may be inferred from a note in his diary for 16 November: "the amendment was rejected, I am glad to say". As Lord Wicklow put it, "granted good will, no paper safeguards are necessary; without it they are useless".[93] But it was the end of the Anti-Partition League: Bernard spoke at the winding-up meeting on 16 February 1923.

The events and circumstances of 1922 had vitiated any developing tradition or organised and united political activity on the part of the southern unionists, and from this on they made little impact on politics either in England or Ireland[94] even though they still believed that they were within the British empire.

All the southern unionists including Bernard held the view (that we can now see to be illusory) that southern Ireland was not by now an independent country and when this belief seemed to be under threat he wrote as follows to Austen Chamberlain MP[95] on 18 February 1924: "I write about rumours that a deal that (a) the Ulster boundary will be undisturbed and (b) that members of the Dáil will not be required to take the oath of allegiance. The real danger is to Irish loyalists who recognise in the Irish government, as is at present constituted, the King's government. Our position would become quite intolerable if we were excluded from the Empire. We were definitely promised that this would not be so at the time of the treaty."

—⁂—

The Provost

THE APPOINTMENT OF Bernard as provost of Trinity College in 1919 surprised many, and some, both at the time and subsequently, were critical of his decision to leave the archbishopric of Dublin for the provostship. One such was Geraldine Fitzgerald, who was assistant librarian of the Royal Irish Academy while Bernard was president (1919–21). In a letter to the writer in 1961 she wrote: "He was a 'proud prelate' certainly and incurred (I think on the whole rightly) much censure for leaving his archbishopric to become provost." Bernard himself must have been aware of the criticism, for he has left in his papers a memorandum setting out in some detail how he came to accept the provostship.[96] The impression has been given that he was imposed on the college as an outsider. This is quite wrong: he was already vice-chancellor and he had been a professor until 1911; in many ways, Trinity College was seen to be an extension of the Church of Ireland, and most of the previous provosts had been clergymen.[97] In any case he was urged by some of the fellows and professors to accept the provostship if it was offered to him: as McDowell and Webb have made clear in their college history, "the field was not at first promising".[98] The only real alternative to Bernard was John Joly, who as a professor and a scientist did not have the support of a majority of the fellows.

As Bernard himself wrote, "at first thought the idea of becoming provost was absurd, but after a fortnight or so I began to see that the offer would probably be made and that I would have to consider it seriously. On May 10, 1919 two of the fellows came to beg me to allow my name to be put forward first and a deputation from the professors came to ask if I would take it. I said to the former that I would not allow my name to be put forward and to the latter that it would be wise for them to concentrate their strength on Professor John Joly whom they had as a 'second string'. My old friend Sir Edward Carson enquired if I would accept the office myself – I said I thought it unlikely that I would accept the provostship but that my experience in 1904 had taught me the folly of even considering alternatives until the offer was before me. The university members of parliament and also the Lord Chancellor (Sir James Campbell) were pressing me all this time to take charge of the college. The plain fact was that the friends of Trinity College realised that their *alma mater* was in a bad way ... academic discipline had become lax under Mahaffy's easy-going regime – the fellowship system had broken down hopelessly, the reputation of the place for learning was going down and (most gravest of all to me) the concept of the college as a home of religion as well as learning was rapidly disappearing. The Divinity school had been persistently snubbed since Traill became provost, the chapel had ceased to be a notable feature of college life and there was a great danger that the college would cease to be the mainstay of the Church. No one could doubt that the next provost would have a great work to do for the Church as well as for the college and the country."

There was also a personal reason for a change: "I found the work of the archbishopric as exacting as it was delightful. It took a great deal out of me and I knew that it could not be many years before I would have to resign it. Was it not better to resign when I could do so with dignity and with the prospect of further usefulness? That the provostship was a better paid office did not (I think) weigh much with me. I had arrived at a stage in life when I was content that I was able to pay my way which I could just manage to do as archbishop. I dreaded the idea of breaking down from overwork and then being obliged to go – my wife felt this strongly."

After such hesitations, "Lord French, the Lord Lieutenant, told me on May 15 at a party at my own house, that he had forwarded my name to the prime minister as his nominee for the provostship. 'But', I said, 'your Excellency never asked me if I would take it'. 'No' was the reply 'because I was afraid you would refuse'. I told him that I was not all sure what I would do and that in any case I would not consider the matter until I had the offer in writing from the prime minister, and I told him the fate of Lord Dudley's nomination in 1904. After Lord French had gone, I told the primate (Dr Crozier) and elicited from him the opinion that it would not at any rate be derogatory to the Church's dignity were I to exchange the archbishopric for the provostship." But it was not a decision lightly made: in his diary for 16 May he noted, "tired and worried greatly about the provostship".[99]

At this juncture he consulted the Archbishop of Canterbury, Randall Davidson. One of the interesting things about this letter is that by this stage he had obviously already decided to accept the provostship if it was offered to him because in his reply on 20 May Davidson wrote, "I do not know Ireland at all and I have no means of forming an independent judgement ... after what you have written I think the balance of my judgement would be in favour of you accepting the provostship, but please realise I base this not on any foundation knowledge of my own but entirely what emerges to my mind from your letter ... I know the value we all attach in England to your aid and I have been looking forward to the help you could give us next year at the Lambeth conference.

"If I am forced to incline the other way it is simply because of the representations you have put before me, although your letter is singularly indeed strikingly impartial in its summing up of the two."[100]

"Nothing then happened, except a good deal of gossip, until June 2 when Mr Bonar Law offered me the provostship in the name of the prime minister. I wrote to accept with a heavy heart and called in the afternoon to tell Lord French. Subsequently, I had a letter from Mr Lloyd George and the thing was announced in the papers on June 7 and I was admitted provost on June 12. Now that I have accepted the office, I feel I have done the right thing. It was no easy task but the overreaching importance for the country as well as the Church reconciled me somewhat to giving up my pastoral staff and all that it means." McDowell and Webb, the college historians, commented that "the slim and handsome young man had become a solid and somewhat stony-faced prelate ... with heaviness of touch and manner went a hardness which made him more respected than loved. There was a wide-spread feeling that Trinity needed a strong man to see it through the difficult days that lay ahead and Bernard certainly was strong ... (He) was a perfectionist, reluctant to delegate; he interfered too often in small details of college admin-istration and soon came to be regarded as an over-meticulous disci-plinarian. In spite of these defects, however, Bernard gave of his best to the college. He worked hard for it and used all his influence on its behalf; he was stern, but did his best to be just; and he behaved steadily and responsibly when the events of 1921 destroyed at once the political ideals for which he had fought and also his hopes of financial prosperity for the college."[101]

First of all, in April 1920 a Royal Commission (the Geikie Commission) appointed to enquire into the finances of Trinity College began its sittings: it recommended a capital grant of £113,000 and an annual grant of £49,000. But this proved to be a false dawn: before the report was even published, the Government of Ireland Bill was introduced and as a result of strenuous lobbying by Bernard a clause giving the college an annual grant of £30,000 was to be chargeable on the exchequer of Southern Ireland. On 1 November 1920 the provost and Sir Robert Woods MP had an inter-view with the Rt Hon. H.A.L. Fisher MP about an amendment to the Government of Ireland Bill which would secure the annual subsidy to Trinity College. £30,000 was a considerable come-down from the £49,000 of the Geikie Commission but even this was not to be paid, as the southern Irish parliament never functioned. When the Anglo-Irish treaty was signed in December 1921 the claims of Trinity College were not included and Lloyd George coolly informed Bernard that the matter had escaped his memory.

It was no use the provost urging on Lloyd George the fact that

Trinity College "was the centre of loyalty and allegiance to the king in this country".[102] Bernard was a frequent and honoured guest at the English and Scottish universities (he was an honorary DCL of Durham and Oxford and an Honorary Fellow of the Queen's College Oxford) and it must have galled him to have to go cap in hand to his new masters, the Free State government.

The years 1922 and 1923 were largely taken up with lobbying by Bernard, first in Whitehall and then with the government of the Irish Free State. Bernard managed to wring some financial concessions out of the new Irish State, but they were small in comparison with what had been recommended by the Geikie Commission. There is among the Bernard papers a memo as to how the promised £30,000 was to be apportioned among the various college debts, but of course it was never received.

In fact, due to Bernard, Trinity received in the years 1919–23 a series of capital grants from the British government totalling £56,000, almost half the capital sum recommended by the Geikie Commission. Of course, TCD considered itself to be a British university, but the comparison with the other federal university in Ireland (which received nothing) is striking. In addition, TCD received from the Free State government a sum of £3,000 p.a. to compensate it for rent losses due to the new Land Act and also two capital sums: £76,000 in the hands of the public trustee originally intended to compensate the college for loss of rental income from compulsory land purchase and £5,000 to relieve individual cases of hardship. These financial concessions required a number of trips to Downing Street on the part of Bernard. On 15 November 1921 the provost, the Earl of Midleton and Andrew Jameson were received by the prime minister and a committee of the cabinet to lay the case of the southern loyalists before the government. At that meeting the provost represented the claim of his college to a subsidy of £30,000 as provided in the Government of Ireland Act (1920) even if that act were to be superseded by another. As we have seen, the plight of the southern loyalists and Trinity College were almost totally ignored in the Anglo-Irish treaty of the following month despite the fact that Bernard received assurances of "the sympathy and good will" of the cabinet on that point.[103] This was pointed out by Bernard in the course of another visit to Downing Street on 7 December. The prime minister merely expressed his regret "that he had overlooked the point but he felt confident that the money would be paid by the new Irish State".[104]

In spite of this, the board of the college, with Bernard in the chair, agreed "to support the terms of settlement for the future government of Ireland already accepted by the British cabinet and by the delegates from Dail Eireann. The true interests of Trinity College can only be furthered by Irish peace and in the building up of happier conditions in Ireland, the board of Trinity College believes that Trinity men should take an active and sympathetic part".[105]

That this statesmanlike acceptance of the rise of Sinn Féin was not acceptable to all graduates is shown by the fact that Bernard had a letter published in the *Irish Times* of 29 April 1922 in which he disowned the speech of Field Marshal Sir Henry Wilson at the TCD dining club in London when the field marshal had bluntly stated, "I don't believe in shaking hands with murderers."[106]

The wisdom of throwing in the lot of the college with the new Irish State was shown when civil war broke out in 1922. On 30 June Free State troops occupied the college at 4.00 a.m. to prevent it being seized by the irregulars; "fierce fighting went on at the Four Courts all day but they were finally surrendered at 4.00 p.m. Sniping from the roofs of houses is a serious danger." [107] On 29 August that year, the college was represented at the funeral of Michael Collins by four senior Fellows headed by the mace – the provost being in Italy.[108]

Bernard was still unwilling to accept the loss of the £30,000 p.a. guaranteed to the college by the Government of Ireland Act (1920) and he had another fruitless interview with the prime minister on 8 February 1922. An indication of the support which the college could still muster at Westminster is shown by the fact that Bernard was accompanied not only by the university's members (Sir Robert Woods and Mr Jellett), but also by Sir Henry Craik MP, Sir Charles Oman MP, Mr J.P. Rawlinson MP, Mr J.A.M. Marriott MP and Sir Martin Conway MP.[109]

Pressure was kept up during 1923. The *Guardian* of 18 May noted a speech by Lord Carson in the House of Lords about the annual grant of £30,000 and said "the college is faced with ruin".[110] On 8 June Bernard received a letter from the prime minister (who was now Stanley Baldwin) to say that a grant of £20,000 for the college would be placed on the supplementary estimates, while later that month the Free State government conceded the financial arrangements which have already been noted.[111]

In fact Bernard had done not at all badly for the college, given the circumstances. In a letter to the Right Hon. D.H. Madden (former vice-chancellor) written on 29 January 1924 he referred to the £20,000 as "a solatium for our disappointments under the Ireland Act of 1920" and went on to say, "broadly speaking I think we have come out of the welter of the last three years better than most of us expected. Certainly much better than I expected."[112]

But there were many other matters requiring the provost's attention. Foremost was the government of the college itself. As long before as the death of Provost Salmon in 1904 reform of the governing body was in the air, and if Bernard had been appointed to succeed him, as the then Lord Lieutenant, the Earl of Dudley, had recommended, Bernard would have been seen as the Liberal candidate. This desire to reform the governing body was furthered by the King's letter of 1911 which allowed for two representatives of the professors and two representatives of the junior Fellows to join the senior Fellows on the board. But the pace of reform quickened when Bernard became provost in 1919.

The ordinance of 1919 which amended drastically the method of election to fellowship was followed by another in 1920 which altered equally drastically the financial conditions of tenure: in effect a newly elected fellow would no longer have to starve until a tutorship became available. He would receive an immediate salary of £440 p.a. and, in return, would have to perform specific teaching duties. Senior Fellows could look forward to receiving the still very substantial income of about £1150 p.a. without any retiring age.

By July 1920 the whole method of election to Fellowship had been recast. In the future Fellows would be elected when required and usually from the ranks of those who were already lecturers or assistants. The theory that the ideal teacher was one who had headed the list of competitors at a severe examination and could show no other qualification for his work had at length been finally rejected.[113] The dominance of the elderly seven senior Fellows on the board of the college was to take much longer to dismantle. What Bernard thought of them is shown by his annotation of the Revd T.T. Gray's laudatory obituary on his death aged 91 in 1924. He wrote: "I knew Gray for almost 50 years. He was not a learned man; he never preached and could not have done so; he did not go to church or chapel for the last 20 years. He was of no use in the divinity school as a lecturer and he did all he could to thwart the will of the professors ... He was very unscrupulous in his methods of opposing those who did not agree with him ... He was very fond of money."[114]

Financial stringency notwithstanding, a number of new academic developments took place during Bernard's provostship. Chairs of Bacteriology and Education were founded in 1921 and a new course in science was instituted. The regulations governing honours degrees in all subjects were revised. Italian and Spanish were added to the modern languages course in 1921 and Irish in 1927 while in 1922 a moderatorship course in oriental languages was instituted. Commerce became a professional school in 1925 and the standard required for a first-class degree was significantly raised. A finance committee was established to manage investments with excellent results.

The number of academic staff in the college in Bernard's time as provost was modest by modern standards: in 1919 there were 31 Fellows, 31 non-Fellow professors (of whom 18 were full-time) and 26 lecturers and assistants. As regards students, there were in 1920 1,026 men and 248 women. At the October entrance in 1924 the number of Roman catholic students were equal to the number of Church of Ireland. Bernard remarked that this was "a significant sign of the times".[115]

A non-academic initiative in 1924 was the gift by the Earl of Iveagh (the chancellor) of the Bath House, which was to transform the lives of resident students over the next forty years. Given Bernard's liking for Latin in all memorials it was perhaps inevitable that the plaque recording this gift should have begun "has balneas

..." A more controversial gift by Lord Iveagh was the large portrait of Bernard by Leo Whelan which provoked Professor N.J.D. White to write his memoir of Bernard "which may modify the impression of him suggested by the portrait that hangs in the Common Room of Trinity College Dublin."[116]

It is the duty of the provost to form part of the caput at commencements and this duty was regularly performed by Bernard not least when honorary degrees were conferred. On 4 July 1919, shortly after Bernard's admission as provost, honorary degrees were conferred on Viscount French of Ypres, the Lord Lieutenant; on General Sir Henry Wilson; and on "others who had distinguished themselves in the war"; and at the commencements dinner that evening Lord French replied to the toast of "the college";[117] while in 1922 when honorary degrees were conferred on, among others, the Earl of Midleton, reality broke in when the public orator's elegant Latin sentences were punctuated by rifle shots from a fierce skirmish which was being fought 300 yards away.[118] In 1924 honorary degrees were offered to "both the King's representatives in Ireland" – Tim Healy and the Duke of Abercorn.[119]

In June 1926 one of the recipients of honorary degrees was Nathan Soderblom, Archbishop of Uppsala, and one of the best known churchmen of his generation. On the preceding Sunday he had preached the university sermon and he had also given the Donnellan lectures on "Erasmus, Loyola and Luther".[120]

The provost presided each Trinity Monday when the names of the new fellows and scholars were announced from the steps of the public theatre; it was on the first such occasion that the undergraduates threw pennies at his feet to demonstrate their view that he had accepted the provostship because the salary was larger than that of the archbishopric – a belief denied by Bernard in his memorandum of his reasons for accepting the provostship. So, what were his relations with the students? Clearly he was not much loved and the college historians have described him as "an over-meticulous disciplinarian",[121] but the account which they give of Bernard's reception of the airman Alcock is contradicted by Bernard's own diary entry for 16 June 1919,[122] when he wrote: "dined in hall, a disgraceful scene of rowdyism as Captain Alcock who had just flown the Atlantic appeared on the scene". However, he appeared at all the things in the college which the provost ought to appear at, for example, on 23 June 1920 he attended the 150th anniversary celebrations of the college's Historical Society which took the form of an inter-university debate followed by a large dinner in the hall. On 7 October 1921 he presided at a meeting in the Regent House to commemorate the sixth centenary of Dante, and he noted that the Lord Lieutenant and Lady Fitz Alan attended.[123] While he preserved among his papers a silk programme for the performance in the Gaiety Theatre by the Dublin University Dramatic Society of a performance of A.A. Milne's comedy *Mr Pim Passes By* held on 8 March 1922 before "their Excellencies the Lord Lieutenant and Lady Fitz Alan".[124]

In 1925 at the opening meeting of the University Philosophical Society he spoke of what a university should stand for: "the ideal of a real university couldn't be narrow. Its scale, its interest, its activities should be world-wide and it should seek and get and give the best, regardless of mere nationality."[125]

A matter on which Bernard and the students were at one was the annual observance of Armistice Day. On 11 November each year silence was observed in the college for two minutes at 11.00 a.m. in memory of the fallen. In 1924 the students spilled out on to College Green where they stopped the traffic. On the evening of Armistice Day 1919 Bernard presided at a service dinner in the dining hall for 230 officers, all of whom were TCD men; the Lord Lieutenant, Lord French, was the principal guest.[126] On Armistice Day 1920 a similar service dinner was held in the hall.[127] While in November 1923 the *Irish Times* noted that the names of no fewer than 454 Trinity men who fell in the great war would be read out.[128] Each year in Trinity week he presided at the College Races; his wife presented the prizes on the first such occasion shortly after his admission as provost. In 1921 Trinity week was cancelled following receipt of threatening letter from the IRA which subsequently claimed that it was a forgery. But in Trinity week 1926 some 300 people attended the provost's garden party to meet the Governor-General, who was now Tim Healy.

It was the duty of the provost to be the public face of the college at many outside functions – something that Bernard was clearly good at. Thus in 1919 and 1920 the provost spoke at dinners of the North of England graduates, while in April 1921 he spoke at the annual dinner of the TCD Dining Club in London, Sir Edward Carson being in the chair. He obviously believed in using these occasions to impart to the graduates the careful political line which the college was treading under his direction. At the Liverpool dinner of the north of England graduates, at which about 150 attended, he said that Trinity College would look with great disfavour on any legislation which would cut off any portion of Ireland, "the remark was received with general applause", and he went on to say, in reply to Lord Killanin, "As regards the political situation he doesn't think the college should take any side or any part Trinity College stood for the whole of the country (hear hear) their business was not a political one – it was simply to help on the higher education of both north and south. They had always had a certain proportion of students of sturdy Presbyterians from the north and a certain proportion of loyal Roman Catholics from the south and he hoped they would always get them (hear hear)."[129]

Becoming provost enabled him to spend more time outside Ireland particularly in London where he was well known and moved in the highest circles. In London he usually stayed either with Lady St Helier at 52 Portland Place or with the Cecil Harmsworths at 28 Montague Square, using the Athenaeum as a sort of day-centre. To take his first 18 months as provost in 1919–20 as an example: on Sunday 6 July 1919, having stayed in bed until 12.30 and having taken over the provost's house from the bursar, he left for London by the night boat and arrived at Lord Midleton's house in Portland Place for breakfast. He plunged straight into the social round: Lady Douro, Lord Vernon, Lady Graham and Sir P. Barton were invited to meet him at lunch and at the Athenaeum in the evening he dined with the Earl and Countess of Desart and also there were the Verneys and Lady Constance Butler and he also met the Earl of Granard and Lord Oranmore and Browne. The next day he called on Sir William McCormack at the University Grants Commission and lunched with Professor Alison Phillips at the Saville Club. That evening Lord and

Lady Midleton held a dinner party for him; present were the Earl of Bessborough, Lord and Lady Barrymore, Lady Edward Cecil, Canon and Mrs Carnegie, Lady Powerscourt and "some men". The following night he attended the bishops' dinner at the Mansion House, Lady Constance Butler accompanying him. The next night he dined with the Harmsworths at the House of Commons and the following day returned to Dublin by the day mail. He notes that on the day after that (12 July) the dean of Wells arrived to stay: he was to preach and lecture at a "clergy week".

After less than a week Bernard was back in London: he left Dublin by the night mail on 17 July having lunched that day at the Viceregal Lodge and spoken at a meeting about a memorial to Irish soldiers. This time he stayed with the Harmsworths and he attended a conference of "university magnates" at the Imperial Institute. He brought his daughter-in-law Lucy to a lord mayor's luncheon for General Pershing of the U.S. army. On 19 July there was the great victory march of troops through London, and one suspects that this was the main reason that he had come: "I could not bring myself to use the seat which the kind Harmsworths had provided for me. But I went down to Whitehall to see the pillar erected 'to the glorious dead' which the troops had saluted. I saluted it too with a full heart."[130]

They had not yet moved from the palace to the provost's house. He arrived home on 21 July 1919 and for 23–24 July noted that men were moving furniture all day. They left the Palace on 24 July, Mrs Bernard going to the Royal Hibernian Hotel and Bernard himself stayed at the University Club. July 26 was spent settling into the provost's house – "hot and fatiguing – we are both tired". On the following day the provost and Mrs Bernard had dinner at the Salthill Hotel in Monkstown at a total cost of £1.2s.0d.

They then left Dublin on holiday which they spent at Huntington Castle, Clonegal. He interrupted it to go up to Dublin by train from Shillelagh on 12 August, returning the following day, after which he had to spend three days in bed: "I got quite knocked out by my journey to Dublin – feverish and tired." By 15 September the holiday was over: "children and nurses got the train from Shillelagh and Maudie and I motored up to the provost's house in time for luncheon". And the usual dinners began. For example, on the following evening he and Mrs Bernard dined with Walter Long, the First Lord of the Admiralty, on the Admiralty yacht at Dun Laoghaire: "Lord French, Lord and Lady Fitzwilliam and a large party were there: very pleasant indeed".

On 16 October it was back to England again. He preached at the commemoration of benefactors in Ely Cathedral and then moved to Oxford, where he stayed at the deanery with Dean Strong. He preached the assize sermon in the university church and dined in the hall of Christ Church. Then on 20 October he presided and spoke at a Dublin University dinner in Manchester which has already been noted.

The whole of November and December were spent in Dublin. He spoke at the opening meetings of both the College Historical Society and the University Philosophical Society and presided at the board: "long and tiresome". A tea party was held for the entire staff "about 80 came". Bishop Montgomery preached a university sermon and a dinner party was held for him on the previous evening while there was an attempt to assassinate Lord French, the Lord Lieutenant, on 20 December. He left for London again on 31 December. He notes that the servants at the end of that year were: butler, under-housemaid, under-parlour maid, kitchen maid, housemaid, lady's maid and cook – by our standards an enormous staff.

Having breakfasted at the Athenaeum he proceeded to the Queen's College, Oxford (of which he was an honorary fellow), and dined at the "needle and thread" dinner at which he sat next to Mr Asquith. The following day he dined in the common room at the Queen's College and then once more travelled to Manchester: "Mr Scott of the Manchester Guardian dined to meet me". He preached morning and evening in the cathedral and then returned to Dublin on 5 January. On 17 February 1920 he married his daughter Alice in the college chapel to Lieutenant Col. George Boase. The Lord Lieutenant signed the register and some 300 guests were entertained in the Provost's House including the Lord Chancellor, the Lord Chief Justice and the Chancellor of the university (the Earl of Iveagh).

The usual round of dinners then ensued; for example, on 25

February he dined at Lord Iveagh's – "a big dinner of 40 men". On 22 March he left for London once more: he and Mrs Bernard stayed at Lady St Helier's and plunged into a round of dinners; for example, on 25 March a dinner at Lord and Lady Midleton's was pronounced "a nice party of 18" – the Duke and Duchess of Devonshire, the Marquess and Marchioness of Salisbury, the Earl and Countess of Pembroke, Lord Iveagh, Lord Windsor. The only serious engagements in this trip were when he made a speech on the Home Rule Bill in the committee room at the House of Commons and spent a day in the record office in Chancery Lane. On 1 April while he was staying at Pepper Harrow he and Lord Midleton settled a political programme for the southern loyalists.

They left for home on 7 April and the expenses of this trip – presumably for two people – came to £19.4s.5d. Having presided at Trinity Monday on 31 May and spoken at the 150th anniversary of the College Historical Society he gave a lecture in St Nicholas Church, Liverpool, on 7 June on 'Dogma and Criticism', having spent most of the previous day (a Sunday) preparing it. Immediately on his return from this overnight engagement Dean Armitage Robinson arrived to give the Donnellan lectures. But he was in London again on 19 June to stay at the deanery, Westminster: he preached in the Abbey and "strolled over to Lambeth to see the Archbishop of Canterbury".

On 21 June he lunched with Lord and Lady Midleton and dined and slept at Rutland Gate with the Earl and Countess of Desart. But he gave evidence at the Irish office before the Union Commission and attended a "little meeting" of unionist peers in the committee room of the House of Lords. The following day he proceeded to Oxford to stay once more with Dean Strong at Christ Church deanery. On 23 June he received the honorary degree of DCL at the encaenia and attended a gaudy at Christ Church – "a very splendid entertainment. Oxford looking its best."

Then it was back to Dublin where he preached and unveiled a war memorial at Clontarf church on Sunday 27 and presided at commencements on 30 June. But by 3 July he was back in London staying at 34 Portland Place even though Lord and Lady Midleton were away. They had returned by 6 July and entertained a large party of 24 to dinner. The next evening he dined at Grillions Club and then on the 8th he and Mrs Bernard travelled to Paris and they did not return to Dublin until 20 September. During this extended continental holiday Bernard was able to complete his work on "the odes of Solomon", but the only reference to Ireland in his diary is for 20 July, when he noted "the Irish news is dreadful – poor country".

Soon after his return he had a long conversation with Stewart and Andrew Jameson about Irish politics while in the course of a dinner at the vice-regal lodge on 15 October he noticed that both the Lord Lieutenant and General Macready were inclined to swear at Greenwood, "who is too often an absentee".

On 16/18 October he was in Liverpool again staying with Bishop and Mrs Chavasse giving the annual sermon for doctors at St Luke's and taking the chair at a dinner of Dublin University graduates which has already been noted. Back he went to Dublin but on 31 October he left again for London and the meeting at the House of Commons with H.A.L. Fisher (in lieu of the prime minister), which has been already noted. Then on 2 November he left London for Co. Durham to join a great house party of 30 at Wynyard Park prior to officiating at the marriage in Durham Cathedral of the Hon. Oliver Stanley to Lady Maureen Stewart: "I suppose 3,000 people were in the cathedral." He arrived back in Dublin at 8.15 a.m. on 6 November just in time for meetings of the senate and the board.

On 27 November he left Dublin again – this time for Oxford, where he preached the university sermon and stayed with the president of Trinity. Then he went on to London staying with Lady St Helier and seeing the Harmsworths and the Midletons returning to Dublin on 2 December – but he left again for London on 21 December; he christened a grandchild at St Mary Abbots and dined at Grillions and seems to have spent the rest of 1920 there. His financial summary for the year 1920 is illuminating:

INCOME:	provost-ship	£2,929.16s.1d
	plus other things making	£3,107.17s.5d total income
EXPENSES:	income tax	£436
	wages	£247

So Bernard busied himself with many and varied occupations. In April 1925 he set off for Canada and the United States where an extensive series of speaking engagements had been arranged for him and the receipt of four honorary degrees. After he had spoken in Montreal, Ottawa and Toronto he was taken ill and had to return to Dublin. Thereafter his health never recovered, although right up to the end he fulfilled the duties of his office. He was compelled to spend the winter of 1926–7 in the south of France but he returned to the college in April "to take up his duties or such of them as his state of health will allow".[131] He presided, as usual, at the announcement of Fellows and Scholars in Trinity Monday but was too ill to attend the dinner that evening. He died of heart failure in the Provost's House on 29 August 1927 at the age of 67, having just completed his great commentary on St John's gospel, which has only recently been superseded in the light of more recent scholarship. Of the many tributes which were paid to him one of the most perceptive is that of Dr Gregg, who followed him in the see of Dublin:

"He was essentially a man of affairs. He had an acute perception of the workings of men's minds and on the practical possibilities to be found in any given situation. While there was a genuine idealism in his sense of what ought to be done he never strayed from a firm realism which perceived what could be done. I believe that it was his practical realism which determined his attitude towards the convention of 1918. Many were distressed at what they considered his defection from pure unionist principles but his political instinct told him that the days of the union were numbered. It was with him a question of what was the best substitute that could be got. To refuse to consider the question at all was a possible policy but he felt that he had something to contribute to the discussion and that it was his business to do it. Nobody I believe wished for political change less than Bernard, but nobody felt more strongly than he that to refuse to help in deliberation was an unpatriotic disloyalty. The convention proved abortive; but his contribution to its deliberations marked him out as one of the leading constructive figures in contemporary Ireland.

"I spoke of his veneration for law and precedent. I think his strong churchmanship was bound up with his sense of continuity. Authority played an important part in his religious outlook ... though he was one whose attitude to practical and speculative questions was largely determined by reason and who distrusted a priori arguments there were nevertheless certain prejudices which caused him in one or two connections to be conservative ... he believed in a fundamental inequality between the sexes and in the pre-determined inferiority of the one sex to the other. He accepted the higher education of women but he did not accept its corollary in their political emancipation. He opposed the extension of the franchise to women in the church. He viewed with scant sympathy the modern demand that a woman should run her own life. For him a woman's place was in the home.

"It is impossible to estimate the influence he exercised on the ministry of the Church of Ireland; about 1,000 of whose members passed through his hands in 23 years. It is there that, in my view, his memorial stands and will stand. To him more than any other man of the last fifty years we owe it that the Church of Ireland is not content with merely being a insular church but is conscious of its continuity with the church of the past and of its place in the Catholic church of today."[132]

The estimate of his erstwhile friend Newport White, by now Regius Professor of Divinity, is more succinct: "He was a born ruler of men and would have made an admirable dictator in Ireland."[133]

The DNB entry gives a very judicious summary of his career. It says: "by Irish standards he ranked as a high churchman – but one entirely untouched by Romanising tendencies. He invited leading figures in the Church of England to St Patrick's; he was a friend of Davidson and Armitage Robinson. He was select preacher at both Oxford and Cambridge", and Archbishop Lang said of him "no one did more to make links of understanding and sympathy between the Church of England and the Church of Ireland".

Many have said that he was unable to communicate with unlettered laymen. But this view is not shared by Thomas Lindsay, one of his oldest and closet friends and later his archdeacon in Dublin, who wrote: "... he would visit a parish, make friends with its chief workers, greet even the humblest with unaffected cordiality and leave them inspired with love for their Church". To him "whatever Bernard did he seemed to do perfectly".[134]

Endnotes

1 She long outlived him, dying in 1940 at Hampton Court Palace where she had been given a grace-and-favour apartment.
2 At his death he had no fewer than thirty titles to his name.
3 R.H. Murray, *Archbishop Bernard* (London 1931), p. 15.
4 Ibid.
5 R.H. Murray, op. cit., p. 52.
6 R.B. McDowell & D.A. Webb, *Trinity College Dublin 1592–1952* (Cambridge 1982), p. 308.
7 TCD MS 11047/18.
8 Ibid.
9 Ibid. This view is contradicted in W.B. Stanford and R.B. McDowell *Mahaffy* (London 1971), p. 253.
10 BL add MS 49804.
11 TCD MS 11047/18.
12 N.J.D. White, *John Henry Bernard* (Dublin 1928), p. 10.
13 TCD MS 10637.
14 Ibid sub 5 February.
15 TCD MS 11047/18.
16 See DNB *sub* Bernard
17 Desart Court was burnt down in 1923 "by Sinn Féin raiders". It was later re-built but subsequently demolished.
18 TCD MS 10645.
19 Ibid.
20 TCD MS 10647.
21 Ibid.
22 The fifth earl succeeded his brother in 1898. He was Director of Public Prosecutions (in London) 1894-1908 and he was a bencher of the Inner Temple.
23 At a visitation the bishop sat in his chair in the cathedral and all the incumbents and churchwardens came up to him parish by parish bringing their registers and the bishop would examine them.
24 Le Fanu was vicar of St John's Sandymount, which was notoriously "High Church".
25 TCD MS 10650.
26 Ibid.

27   Shelton Abbey is now a prison. Previously it was a hotel run by the last Earl of Wicklow.

28   Fortunately the house was large: it is now the Cashel Palace Hotel.

29   He was incumbent of Castlemacadam 1886–1921.

30   This was the 6th earl of Portarlington; his seat Emo Court is now owned by the State.

31   TCD MS 1065.

32   Ibid.

33   This was a meeting of the diocesan synod to elect a new bishop of Cashel.

34   The house became a hotel after the death there of the 7th earl of Donoughmore in 1981.

35   Susan Lady St Helier DBE was the widow of the first and last Baron St Helier who died in 1905. She was the mother of Lady Midleton.

36   Coolcarrigan is still lived in by the Wilson-Wrights. It is a large estate near Carbury, Co. Kildare. The private chapel in the grounds functions as a parish church for the local area.

37   See Patrick Buckland, *Irish Unionism 1885–1923* (Belfast 1973), p. xv.

38   Walter Hume Long 1854–1924, Chief Secretary for Ireland, 1905–6. His mother was the daughter of an Irish MP and in 1878 he married a daughter of the 9th Earl of Cork and Orrery. He was given a peerage in 1921 after holding a number of posts in the government. See John Kindle *Walter Long, Ireland and the Union 1905-20* (Dublin 1992).

39   TCD MS 2388/93/990.

40   BL add. MS 52782.6.

41   BL add. MS 52782.10.

42   BL add. MS 52782.13.

43   BL add. MS 52782.15.

44   TCD MS 10644.

45   Edward Henry Carson (1854–1935). He was created a peer in 1921.

46   TCD MS 10646.

47   BL add. MS 52782.43.

48   BL add. MS 52784.

49   BL add. MS 52782.48.

50   TCD MS 2388/93/989.

51   A Roman Catholic bishop.

52   Ibid.

53   TCD MS 2388-93.965.

54   A former Chief Secretary for Ireland and a former prime minister.

55   BL add. MS 52782/75.

56   TCD MS 10648.

57   Ibid.

58   *National Review*, March–August 1916.

59   BL add. MS 52781.

60   DNB sub Carson.

61   BL add. MS 5281.
62   Ibid.
63   BL MS 52782.129.
64   BL MS 52782.137.
65   BL add. MS 52782.139.
66   BL add. MS 52781.
67   BL add. MS 52782.150.
68   BL add. MS 52782.156.
69   BL add. MS 2388/93.997.
70   Buckland, *Irish Unionism*, pp 350–51.
71   McDowell, *The Irish Convention 1917–18* (London 1970), p. 90.
72   TCD MS 2388.128.
73   McDowell, op.cit., p. 146.
74   TCD MS 10649.
75   TCD MS 10649.
76   BL add. MS 52784.
77   McDowell, op. cit., p. 127.
78   BL add. MS 52781.
79   BL add. MS 52781.26.
80   Ibid.
81   Buckland, op. cit., pp. 360, 361.
82   BL add. MS 52781.
83   TCD MS 2388/161.
84   Buckland, *Irish Unionism I: the Anglo-Irish and the new Ireland 1885–1913* (Dublin 1972), pp 192–201. See also R.B. McDowell *Crisis and decline: the fate of the southern unionists* (Dublin 1998).
85   TCD MS 2388/172.
86   BL add. MS 52783.
87   Ibid.
88   BL add. MS 52783.
89   Ibid.
90   TCD MS 10652.
91   Ibid.
92   BL add MS 52783.
93   R.H. Murray, op. cit., p. 293.
94   Buckland, *Irish Unionism I*, p. 296.
95   Austen Chamberlain became foreign secretary in November 1924.
96   TCD MS 11047/18.
97   As provost Bernard always wore the frock coat and gaiters of an Anglican dignitary and he chose to be painted by Leo Whelan in the rochet and chimere of a bishop rather than in academic dress.
98   McDowell & Webb, p. 423.
99   TCD MS 10651.
100 TCD MS 11047/17

101 McDowell & Webb, pp 424–5.
102 Letter from the provost to the prime minister. Board Register 29 October 1921. For a fuller discussion of this matter see Robert MacCarthy, *The Trinity College Estates 1800–1923* (Dundalk 1992), pp 85–6.
103 TCD MS 2381.
104 Ibid.
105 BM 12 December 1921.
106 TCD MS 2381.
107 Ibid.
108 Ibid.
109 Ibid.
110 Ibid.
111 Ibid.
112 TCD MS 2386.
113 TCD MS 2381.
114 TCD MS 2386.
115 TCD MS 2381.
116 N.J.D. White, *John Henry Bernard* (Dublin 1928), p. 2.
117 TCD MS 2381.
118 Ibid.
119 Ibid. But the Duke of Abercorn said that it would be unsafe for him to receive the degree in Dublin in person (BL add. MS 52783).
120 Ibid.
121 McDowell & Webb, op. cit., pp 424–5.
122 TCD MS 10651.
123 TCD MS 2381.
124 TCD MS 2386.
125 *Irish Times* 6 November 1925.
126 TCD MS 2381.
127 Ibid.
128 Ibid.
129 *Liverpool Courier* 19 October 1920.
130 TCD MS 10651.
131 TCD MS 2381.
132 R.H. Murray, *Archbishop Bernard*, pp 234–5.
133 N.J.D. White, *Some Recollections of Trinity College Dublin* (Dublin 1935), p. 24.
134 T.S. Lindsay, *Some Archbishops of Dublin* (Dublin 1928), pp 34–7.

—◊—